**AA**

# 50 WALKS IN

# Wiltshire

## 50 WALKS OF 2–10 MILES

First published 2002
Researched and written by David Hancock
Field checked and updated 2009 by Nick
Channer, David Foster and Nick Reynolds

Commissioning Editor: Sandy Draper
Senior Editor: Penny Fowler
Designer: Tracey Butler
Picture Research: Alice Earle
Proofreader: Marilynne Lanng
Cartography provided by the Mapping
Services Department of AA Publishing

Produced by AA Publishing
© AA Media Limited 2009

Published by AA Publishing (a trading
name of AA Media Limited, whose
registered office is Fanum House, Basing
View, Basingstoke, Hampshire RG21 4EA;
registered number 06112600)

**Enabled by** **Ordnance Survey** This product includes
mapping data licensed
from the Ordnance Survey® with the
permission of the Controller of Her
Majesty's Stationery Office. © Crown
Copyright 2009. All rights reserved. Licence
number 100021153.

A03628

ISBN: 978-0-7495-6297-7
ISBN: 978-0-7495-6330-1

Visit AA Publishing at theAA.com/bookshop

Cover reproduction by Keenes
Group, Andover
Printed by Printer Trento Srl, Italy

Acknowledgements
The Automobile Association wishes to
thank the following photographers and
organisations for their assistance in the
preparation of this book.

Cover: White Horse, Westbury, AA World
Travel Library/Michael Moody

Photography by AA World Travel Library/
Michael Moody

Illustrations by Andrew Hutchinson

Every effort has been made to trace the
copyright holders, and we apologise in
advance for any unintentional omissions
or errors. We would be pleased to apply
any corrections in the following edition
of this publication.

Author Acknowledgement
The author would like to thank Bonita
Toms and Lucy Piper who assisted in
check-walking some of the routes, and
the staff at Bradford-on-Avon, Devizes,
Malmesbury, Marlborough and Salisbury
tourist information centres for their
invaluable assistance.

of fitness. However, all outdoor activities
involve a degree of risk and the publishers
accept no responsibility for any injuries
caused to readers whilst following these
walks. For more advice on walking safely
see page 144. The mileage range shown
on the front cover is for guidance only –
some walks may be less than or exceed
these distances.

*Right: The view from Oare Hill (Walk 10)*

**AA**

**50** WALKS IN

# Wiltshire

50 WALKS OF 2–10 MILES

# Contents

# Contents

## Rating

Each walk is rated for its relative difficulty compared to the other walks in this book. Walks marked ✚ ✚ ✚ are likely to be shorter and easier with little total ascent. The hardest walks are marked ✚ ✚ ✚ .

## Walking in Safety

For advice and safety tips see page 144.

# Locator Map

# Legend

| | | | | |
|---|---|---|---|---|
| ▬▬→▬▬ | Walk Route | | | Built-up Area |
| ❶ | Route Waypoint | | | Woodland Area |
| – – – – | Adjoining Path | | 🚻 | Toilet |
| ☀ | Viewpoint | | 🅿 | Car Park |
| • | Place of Interest | | 🛏 | Picnic Area |
| ⌂ | Steep Section | | )( | Bridge |

# Introducing Wiltshire

A land shrouded in mystery, myth and legend, Wiltshire evokes images of ancient stone circles, white chalk horses carved into hillsides, crop circles and the forbidden, empty landscape of Salisbury Plain. To many M4 and A303 travellers heading out of London through the clutter of the Thames Valley, Wiltshire is where the landscape opens out and rural England begins.

## Wiltshire Landscapes

Wiltshire's charm lies in the beauty of its countryside. The expansive chalk landscapes of the Marlborough and Pewsey downs and Cranborne Chase inspire a sense of space and freedom, offering miles of uninterrupted views deep into Dorset, Somerset and the Cotswolds. South Wiltshire offers the crystal waters of the Ebble, Avon, Nadder and Wylye rivers meandering through tranquil valleys etched into the chalk, linking picture-postcard villages, on their way to Salisbury and its majestic cathedral. Jurassic limestone forms the county's north-west border. This is the south-east edge of the Cotswolds, characterised by its gently undulating landscape and the distinctive, honey-coloured stone buildings.

## Ancient Routes

Although famous the world over for the prehistoric sites of Avebury and Stonehenge, Wiltshire has much more to offer the walker who is keen to explore the 2,500 miles (4,022km) of public footpaths that criss-cross the county. Several long-distance trails pass through Wiltshire, including the Ridgeway, the Thames Path and the Macmillan Way. The circular White Horse Trail visits all Wiltshire's white chalk horses in its 90 miles (145km), and the circular, 30-mile (48km) Imber Range Perimeter Path circumnavigates the army's training area on Salisbury Plain.

Many of the routes described in this book traverse sweeping chalk downlands in search of ancient paths, barrows, monoliths and hill-forts, and the best views. You can stride across the sarsen-strewn landscape of Fyfield Down near Marlborough, walk in the footsteps of Civil War soldiers on Roundway Down above Devizes, and locate two of Wiltshire's famous White Horses on Milk Hill and Westbury Hill. Some walks combine invigorating hilltops with tranquil valleys and riverside strolls or tow path walking beside the Kennet and Avon Canal.

## Settlements

Wiltshire's thriving markets towns and picturesque villages provide interesting starting points and welcome diversions along the way. Stroll through quaint timbered and thatched villages in the southern Woodford and Avon valleys and explore the historic streets of the stone villages of Lacock, Castle Combe and Sherston. Walk around Salisbury and discover architectural

**PUBLIC TRANSPORT**

Wiltshire's good network of bus and rail services provides a convenient way of accessing the county's market towns, villages and tourist attractions. Walks 2, 11, 46, 48/49 and 50 start close to railway stations. For train times call the 24-hour national train information line on 08457 48 49 50. For details of the wide range of public transport services across the county, call the Wiltshire Traveline 0871 200 22 33. You can also get travel information on the internet at www.transportdirect.info.

styles from the 13th century to the present and take time to visit the city's elegant cathedral and fascinating museums. At Devizes, trace the medieval street pattern and admire some grand buildings before following the Kennet and Avon Canal tow path to the famous Caen Hill flight of 29 locks.

## Visitor Attractions

Wiltshire is richly endowed with manor houses, mansions and beautiful gardens. On these walks, you can stroll past Bowood House, Longleat House, Lacock Abbey and Corsham Court, and enjoy a walk between The Courts at Holt and Great Chalfield Manor. Among the impressive gardens, Stourhead stands out, as one of England's finest 18th-century landscaped gardens.

This guide should help you to discover that Wiltshire offers some of the best walking to be found anywhere in lowland, rural England.

# Using this book

### Information panels

An information panel for each walk shows its relative difficulty (see page 5), the distance and total amount of ascent. An indication of the gradients you will encounter is shown by the rating ▲ ▲ ▲ (no steep slopes) to ▲ ▲ ▲ (several very steep slopes).

### Maps

There are 30 maps, covering 40 of the walks. Some walks have a suggested option in the same area. The information panel for these walks will tell you how much extra walking is involved. On short-cut suggestions the panel will tell you the total distance if you set out from the start of the main walk. Where an option returns to the same point on the main walk, just the distance of the loop is given. Where an option leaves the main walk at one point and returns to it at another, then the distance shown is for the whole walk. The minimum time suggested is for reasonably fit walkers and doesn't allow for stops. Each walk has a suggested map.

### Start Points

The start of each walk is given as a six-figure grid reference prefixed by two letters indicating which 100km square of the National Grid it refers to. You'll find more information on grid references on most Ordnance Survey maps.

### Dogs

We have tried to give dog owners useful advice about how dog friendly each walk is. Please respect other countryside users. Keep your dog under control, especially around livestock, and obey local bylaws and other dog control notices.

### Car Parking

Many of the car parks suggested are public, but occasionally you may find you have to park on the roadside or in a lay-by. Please be considerate when you leave your car, ensuring that access roads or gates are not blocked and that other vehicles can pass safely.

*Right: The Westbury White Horse (Walk 45)*

WALK 1

# Border Paths Around the Chutes

*Explore the hills and combes close to the Wiltshire–Hampshire border.*

---

**DISTANCE** *8 miles (12.9km)*  **MINIMUM TIME** *4hrs 15min*

**ASCENT/GRADIENT** *1,099ft (335m)* ▲▲▲  **LEVEL OF DIFFICULTY** +++

**PATHS** *Bridle paths, downland tracks, field paths, roads, 8 stiles*

**LANDSCAPE** *Farmland, woodland, downland pasture, village streets*

**SUGGESTED MAP** *OS Explorer 131 Romsey, Andover & Test Valley*

**START/FINISH** *Grid reference: SU 308530*

**DOG FRIENDLINESS** *Keep dogs under control at all times*

**PARKING** *Lower Chute Club*

**PUBLIC TOILETS** *None on route*

---

This walk explores the hilly and relatively deserted border country between Wiltshire and Hampshire, in what remains of Chute Forest. In medieval times vast tracts of woodland canopied an area stretching from Savernake Forest in the north to Salisbury in the south, before swelling out again into the New Forest, providing a prime hunting ground.

## The Chutes

The parishes of Chute and Chute Forest can be traced back to Norman times. It is believed that the ancient meaning of Chute is wood or forest. Habitation within the parishes at that time was probably no more than a few cottages in a large clearing occupied by charcoal burners or peasants. Deforestation began in 1632 under Charles I (1600–49), who divided the area up among his favoured nobles. The result of this is still evident today in the form of five small hamlets – Upper and Lower Chute, Chute Standen, Chute Forest and Chute Cadley – which developed around what were once farms or country houses, such as Standen House and Chute Lodge.

The landscape is still well wooded with a mixture of copse, plantations, windbreaks or 'rows' and roadside plantings of beech linked by a sprinkling of hedgerow trees. The paths and byways on this walk explore in depth this quite remote area of Wiltshire, which rises to over 800ft (244m), giving splendid views south across Hampshire to the Isle of Wight.

The highest point of the walk is on the impressive Chute Causeway, originally part of the Roman highway from Winchester in Hampshire to Mildenhall, near Marlborough. It forms a great arc around some of the most attractive scenery in Wiltshire, for just north of the now paved road are deep combes (such as Hippenscombe Bottom) and steep hills (such as Knolls Down). Even the Roman road, which usually ignores natural obstacles, swerves to avoid them. At the eastern end of the Causeway is Conholt House, a large, early 19th-century grey-brick building. It was here during excavations in 1898, that a small terrace set with 12–16 inches (30–41cm) of flint was uncovered. Part of this terrace appears to have been burned, which offers an explanation as to how the Romans built such

# THE CHUTES

straight roads — by lighting fires at both ends of the semi-circular section of the Causeway they could line up the columns of smoke to align their road.

## WALK 1 DIRECTIONS

**1** Turn left out of the car park and then right at the T-junction. Fork left at the war memorial, then turn left again by the 'Chute Cadley' village sign. Keep left and take the bridle path, a track, through the edge of woodland.

Continue between hedgerows and descend into Chute Standen.

**2** Turn right at the T-junction then, where the lane swings left to Standen House, keep straight on up a grassy track of Breach Lane. At the T-junction, turn right and then left along the edge of

11

**WALK 1**

### WHAT TO LOOK OUT FOR

Explore Knolls Down and the ramparts of Fosbury Ring, an oval bivallate hill-fort from the Iron Age with views west along Hippenscombe Bottom into the heart of Wiltshire.

woodland. Continue for 0.5 mile (800m) to Chute Causeway.

**3** Cross straight over the causeway and later steeply descend the track to a metalled lane in Hippenscombe Bottom. Turn left, then right and swing right, then left between farm buildings. Fork right along a grassy track (passing to the right of a long, breeze-block barn), which soon swings left and steadily ascend to a crossing of ways.

**4** Turn sharp right along the gravel track. At Fosbury Farm, bear right and walk beside woodland. Follow the track into the woods and, as you leave the woods, briefly leave the marked route to pass through the ancient earthworks into Fosbury Ring on top of Knolls Down.

**5** Fork left on a grassy track never far from the woodland. Pass to the right of a tiny screened pond, then swing left, exit the ring and walk down the left-hand field-edge. Go through the gap in the corner and go around the left edge of a large field. Descend to a cottage in the corner. Turn right along the lane and cross

### WHERE TO EAT AND DRINK

Time your walk to coincide with opening time at the Hatchet Inn in Lower Chute, a thatched 16th-century pub with low beams, a log fire and home-cooked food. Along the way, try the George Inn in Vernham Dean for Greene King ales and traditional pub food.

the stile (perhaps hidden) almost immediately on your left. Keep to the right-hand field-edge to a stile and lane and turn right into Vernham Dean.

**6** Take the waymarked fenced track beside a house called Underwood. The fencing on the right ends just before a gap; here turn right along a hedged track. Follow the track just within woodland, then follow the waymarkers carefully, steeply uphill across a field and through a small plantation to a stile. Turn left along the top of the escarpment to a gate in near the corner and the road.

### WHILE YOU'RE THERE

Visit the ruins of Ludgershall Castle, built during the late 11th century and later used by Henry III. It fell into decay around the 16th century but you can still see some of the original large Norman earthworks.

**7** Turn right then, where the road swings sharp left by a junction, keep straight on over a stile. Initially head towards a barn, but then fork left across a depression and continue to another stile. Cross the next field to a stile and walk down a track between fields. Bear slightly left, then walk along the right-hand field-edge to enter a long, narrow field, bounded by woodland.

**8** Keep to the right-hand edge and go by a redundant stile on the right just before the corner. Continue beside woodland, soon joining a drive which becomes a metalled lane. Turn right at the T-junction and go forward (not forking right) to retrace your steps back to the car park.

# Great Bedwyn and the Kennet and Avon Canal

*Combine a walk beside the Kennet and Avon Canal with a visit to Wiltshire's only working windmill and the beam engines at Crofton.*

---

**DISTANCE** 6.75 miles (10.9km)   **MINIMUM TIME** 2hrs

**ASCENT/GRADIENT** 147ft (45m) ▲▲▲   **LEVEL OF DIFFICULTY** ✦✦✦

**PATHS** Field paths, woodland tracks, tow path, roads, 3 stiles

**LANDSCAPE** Farmland, woodland, canal and village scenery

**SUGGESTED MAP** OS Explorer 157 Marlborough & Savernake Forest

**START/FINISH** Grid reference: SU 279645

**DOG FRIENDLINESS** Dogs can be off lead along tow path

**PARKING** Great Bedwyn Station

**PUBLIC TOILETS** Crofton Pumping Station, portaloo at Wilton Windmill

---

Situated beside a peaceful stretch of the Kennet and Avon Canal, the large village of Great Bedwyn was formerly a market town, with borough status from the 11th century until the Reform Act of 1832 – it even returned two Members of Parliament. It still has the appearance of a small town with a wide main street, continuous rows of cottages, a few elegant town houses and the flint Church of St Mary the Virgin, one of the largest and finest churches in the area, set in low-lying land near to the canal.

## Kennet and Avon Canal

Undeniably, the main reason most visitors come to Great Bedwyn is to enjoy the sights and sounds of the Kennet and Avon Canal and the beautiful scenery it meanders through south-west of the village. It was in 1788 that the idea of linking the River Kennet, which flows into the Thames at Reading, with the River Avon at Bath by means of an artificial waterway was first mooted. The navigation between the rivers had to rise to 450ft (137m) and then descend on the other side and needed 104 locks, two aqueducts and, at the summit, a tunnel over 500yds (457m) long. Construction on the ambitious project, designed by John Rennie (1761–1821), started in 1794 and was completed in 1810. The canal was used to carry vast quantities of coal from the Somerset coalfield, iron, stone and slate, local agricultural products and timber, and to bring luxuries like tobacco and spirits from London to Bath, Bristol and the intervening towns.

## Decline and Restoration

Transporting goods along the canal proved successful for 40 years but then, with the completion of the railways offering faster and more efficient transport, the canal began to fall into decline. Since 1962 the Kennet and Avon Canal Trust and British Waterways have revitalised the navigable waterway by clearing the waters and locks for leisure barges and making the banks and tow paths accessible to anglers, naturalists and walkers.

Also part of the restoration scheme, and the highlight of your walk along the tow path, are the magnificent beam engines at Crofton Pumping Station.

# GREAT BEDWYN

The two beam engines, the 1812 Boulton and Watt and the 1845 Harvey of Hale, operate a huge cast-iron beam and were used to raise water from Wilton Water to the summit level of the canal. Beautifully restored and powered by steam from a hand-stoked, coal-fired Lancashire boiler, you may be lucky to see them working if you're visiting on a summer weekend.

## Wilton Windmill

The county's only complete surviving working windmill stands proudly on a chalk hilltop overlooking the canal. Built in 1821, after the construction of the canal had diverted the water previously used to power mills, it is a five-storey brick tower mill and was fully operational until the 1890s. It closed and became derelict in the 1920s. Restored in the 1970s and floodlit at night, you can once again see local corn being ground into flour.

## WALK 2 DIRECTIONS

**①** Walk to the main road in Great Bedwyn. Turn right, then left down Church Street. Pass Lloyd's Stone Museum and the church, then take the footpath left between two graveyards. Climb a stile, cross a field to a kissing gate, then carefully cross the railway line to another kissing gate. Cross the footbridge, then the bridge over the Kennet and Avon Canal and descend to the tow path.

> **WHAT TO LOOK OUT FOR**
>
> In St Mary's Church, Great Bedwyn, look for the tomb of Sir John Seymour in the chancel. His daughter Jane was Henry VIII's third and best-loved wife.

**②** Turn right, pass beneath the bridge and continue along the tow path for 1.5 miles (2.4km), passing three locks and 2 stiles, to reach Lock 60. Cross the canal here, turn left, then follow a path right and pass through the tunnel beneath the railway. Ascend steps to the Crofton Pumping Station.

**③** Retrace your steps back to the tow path and Lock 60. Turn left for a few paces, then take the footpath right, waymarked to Wilton Windmill, and walk beside Wilton Water along the edge of fields. Eventually, turn right down a short track to a lane by the village pond in Wilton.

> **WHERE TO EAT AND DRINK**
>
> Great Bedwyn has two pubs, the Cross Keys and the Three Tuns, and a bakery. Light refreshments are available if visiting the Crofton Beam Engines, while at Wilton the homely Swan Inn offers meals made with locally sourced produce, snacks, good Sunday lunches and a selection of real ales.

**④** Turn left, then just past the Swan Inn, follow the lane left and uphill through trees. Climb out of the village and fork right to pass Wilton Windmill. Continue along the lane and turn left on to a track, opposite the lane to Hungerford. Just before the wooded track snakes downhill, turn right along a bridle path (unsigned) beside woodland.

**⑤** At a staggered crossing of paths, turn right, then in 50yds (46m), turn left. Go down a well-surfaced track and through a gate into Bedwyn Brail. Continue though the woods, following signs to Great Bedwyn. Go straight across a clearing before forking left to re-enter the woods in the left-hand corner of the clearing.

**⑥** On emerging in a field corner, keep left along the field boundary. Go through a gap in the hedge and descend along the left-hand side of the next field, with Great Bedwyn visible ahead. Near the bottom of the field, bear half right, downhill to the canal.

**⑦** Pass through a gate by a bridge and Lock 64 and turn right along the tow path. Go through the car park to the road, then turn left over the canal and rail bridges before turning right back to Great Bedwyn Station.

> **WHILE YOU'RE THERE**
>
> Visit Lloyd's Stone Museum in Great Bedwyn, a fascinating little open-air museum that demonstrates the art of stonemasonry. Here you can see monuments, gravestones and sculpture dating back to the 18th century. Just north of Great Bedwyn is Chisbury Camp, an ancient hill-fort with the ruins of a 13th-century chapel standing within its 50ft (15m) high earth ramparts.

*Overleaf: Thatched cottages in Great Bedwyn (Walk 2)*

# Savernake's Royal Forest

*A walk through an ancient forest landscape
and beside a tranquil canal.*

| | |
|---|---|
| DISTANCE | 9 miles (14.5km) |
| MINIMUM TIME | 3hrs 30min |
| ASCENT/GRADIENT | 213ft (65m) ▲▲▲ |
| LEVEL OF DIFFICULTY | +++ |
| PATHS | Woodland tracks, tow path, bridle paths, country lanes, 10 stiles |
| LANDSCAPE | Forest, farmland, canal |
| SUGGESTED MAP | OS Explorer 157 Marlborough & Savernake Forest |
| START/FINISH | Grid reference: SU 215646 |
| DOG FRIENDLINESS | Parts of Savernake Forest have signs requesting dogs be kept on lead. Off lead along tow path |
| PARKING | Hat Gate 8 picnic area off A346 south of Marlborough |
| PUBLIC TOILETS | None on route |

On a chalk plateau above Marlborough on the north-east edge of Salisbury Plain, Savernake consists of 2,300 acres (931.5ha) of mixed woodland managed by the Forestry Commission. In the Middle Ages, it was a wilderness of bracken and heathland and had been a royal hunting ground from long before the Norman Conquest. It was William the Conqueror who appointed the first hereditary warden, Richard Esturmy, and subsequent kings of England hunted deer in the forest glades.

## The Seymours

In the 15th century a daughter of the Esturmy family married into the Seymour family who then became wardens of Savernake. In 1535, Jane Seymour was introduced to King Henry VIII while he was hunting with her father, Sir John, in the forest. Local tradition has it that Henry VIII married Jane at Savernake. Jane's brother, Edward Seymour, became warden in 1536 and was created Protector of the Realm, the Duke of Somerset, on Henry VIII's death in 1547. He persuaded Henry's successor King Edward to transfer the ownership of Savernake to the Seymour family. In 1676 it passed by marriage to the Bruce family and so to the present owner, the Marquis of Ailesbury, whose mansion, Tottenham House, was begun in 1781 by the first Earl of Ailesbury.

## Eighteenth-century Landscaping

Although a large part of the forest was enclosed during the early 17th century, much of it decayed due to the lack of replanting following increased timber demands for shipbuilding. Few trees were declared fit for building use by a naval surveyor in 1675. Today's forest was the inspiration of landscape gardener 'Capability' Brown. He planned the 4-mile (6.4km) Grand Avenue that cuts north to south, and the eight lesser beech avenues leading to the forest centre. Originally intended to be formal, it now has an air of informality, with young broad-leaved trees and tall pines intermingling with the surviving great beeches and ancient pollarded oaks.

Great Bedwyn

St Katharine's Church

Tottenham House

170 ▲

197 ▲

GRAND AVENUE

Durley

Savernake Forest

Terrace Hill

195 ▲

Bruce Tunnel

The Column

A346

153 ▲

Leigh Hill

Burbage Wharf

Old Milestone

Hat Gate

A346

Dismantled Railway Bridges

Cadley Lock

175 ▲

Dismantled Railway

MUD LANE

175 ▲

Kennet and Avon Canal

Royal Oak Inn

Wootton Rivers

St Andrew's Church

0        ½ mile

0                1km

## WALK 3 DIRECTIONS

WALK 3

**①** From the car park, turn right, then almost immediately left past a wooden barrier. Follow the wooded path for 500yds (457m), then bear right to reach the A346. Cross over near an old milestone and take the track beyond a wooden barrier, signed to Tottenham House.

**②** In 150yds (137m), at a major crossing of routes, turn right and, after a similar distance, keep left at a junction where the path runs straight on. Follow this straight track (which can be very muddy in places) for 0.75 mile (1.2km) to The Column.

**③** Approaching it, turn left and follow the track to a junction with Grand Avenue. Turn right and follow it to the road. Turn left, pass Warren Lodge and take the next right turning for St Katharine's Church.

**④** Beyond the church turn right at the sign for Durley. Pass through trees and beyond a gate, bear right to a drive, crossing it to a stile beyond the woodland.

Cross parkland and woodland and the drive to Tottenham House and continue to the road.

**⑤** Turn left, walk through the hamlet of Durley and keep to the lane across the old railway bridge, then the main railway bridge, and shortly take the footpath on the right, waymarked 'Wootton Rivers'. You are now walking above the Kennet and Avon Canal as it passes through the Bruce Tunnel.

**⑥** Walk down some steps, pass through a narrow and low tunnel under the railway line and join the canal tow path just below the entrance to the Bruce Tunnel. Turn left along the tow path for about 1.5 miles (2.4km), passing beneath the A346 at Burbage Wharf to reach Cadley Lock.

**⑦** Turn right over bridge No 105 and follow the metalled track to a T-junction. Turn right and keep to the road, passing two dismantled railway bridges, back to the car park at Hat Gate.

# Wootton Rivers

*Continue along the tow path to Wootton Rivers and a charming pub.*
**See map and information panel for Walk 3**

---

**DISTANCE** *11.75 miles (18.9km)*    **MINIMUM TIME** *4hrs*

**ASCENT/GRADIENT** *279ft (85m)* ▲▲▲    **LEVEL OF DIFFICULTY** +++

---

## WALK 4 DIRECTIONS
### (Walk 3 Option)

At Point **7**, don't cross the bridge, instead keep to the canal tow path and pass three further locks to reach bridge No 108 at Wootton Rivers. Leave the tow path and turn right across the bridge into the village.

The section of the Kennet and Avon Canal from Wootton Rivers to the western portal of the Bruce Tunnel includes the Wootton Rivers flight of four locks, which raise the canal 35ft (11m) to its summit level of 450ft (137m) compared to 65ft (20m) in Bath. Beyond the 502ft (153m) long Bruce Tunnel and Crofton Pumping Station, the canal descends gradually all the way to the Thames at Reading.

Wootton Rivers is a classic Wiltshire village. Essentially a linear settlement, it is particularly pretty with its mile-long (1.6km) main street composed almost entirely of timber-framed, thatched cottages and brick houses.

As you stroll gently uphill away from the canal and its restored lock and keeper's cottage, take the long enclosed pathway on your left to visit St Andrew's Church, which stands close to the impressive manor house. Of particular interest is the clock in the wooden belfry. Built in 1911 to commemorate the Coronation of George V, it is unique in having three faces, two are conventional, the third displays the words 'Glory be to God' around the edge of the dial instead of numerals. It was designed by the amusingly named Jack Spratt, an eccentric countryman and amateur clockmaker, out of donations of mechanical junk, old prams, bicycles and bedsteads as the people of the village could not afford to buy one. It is said to have a repertoire of 24 chimes.

Pass St Andrew's Church, Point **A**, on your left and the Royal Oak Inn on your right then, as the road swings right, take the waymarked bridle path left by the house called Martinsell. Follow this tree-lined track, which gently climbs to a T-junction of routes at the top of the hill. Turn right then, in the field corner, turn left and in 50yds (46m) join the track on your right. Turn left and ascend to a further T-junction, Point **B**. Turn right down Mud Lane, a wooded track, eventually reaching a metalled lane in 0.5 mile (800m). Turn left along the lane back to Hat Gate car park.

# Ramsbury and a Murder

*A gentle walk through the tranquil Kennet Valley to Littlecote House.*

| | |
|---|---|
| DISTANCE 6.5 miles (10.4km) | MINIMUM TIME 2hrs |
| ASCENT/GRADIENT 229ft (70m) ▲▲▲ | LEVEL OF DIFFICULTY ✦✦✦ |

PATHS Field paths and established tracks

LANDSCAPE Farmland, woodland, parkland, village streets

SUGGESTED MAP OS Explorers 157 Marlborough & Savernake; 158 Newbury & Hungerford

START/FINISH Grid reference: SU 274715 (on Explorer 157)

DOG FRIENDLINESS Keep dogs under control at all times

PARKING Ample roadside parking in Ramsbury

PUBLIC TOILETS None on route

## WALK 5 DIRECTIONS

The large old village of Ramsbury nestles on a wide stretch of the River Kennet close to the Berkshire border. Between AD 908 and 1058 Ramsbury was the centre of a flourishing diocese, complete with cathedral and bishop, before it was transferred to preferred Sherborne and later to Old Sarum. Although a mere parish for more than nine centuries, the village has an impressive church built on Anglo-Saxon foundations. The many fine Jacobean and Georgian buildings include most notably Ramsbury Manor, a handsome brick building of nine bays, built in 1680 by John Webb, son-in-law of Inigo Jones, which takes advantage of its fine riverside setting. It was in this house that Oliver Cromwell (1599–1658) laid his plans for the subjugation of Ireland.

From the Square and the Bell Inn, take Scholards Lane signed to Hungerford. At The Knap turn right, signed 'Froxfield', cross the River Kennet and, just before a cottage, take the metalled track left, waymarked to Littlecote House. As the drive bears right, continue straight on along a track through the valley. In 0.5 mile (800m), pass a cottage called West Lodge, and enter a field. Keep left along the field-edge, eventually passing the remains of a Roman villa.

William George, the steward of Littlecote Park, unearthed the remains of the villa, including a large mosaic floor, in the early 18th century. Edward Popham, the owner of Littlecote, allowed George to make detailed drawings of the mosaic before ordering

### WHILE YOU'RE THERE

Follow the walk with a leisurely drive to the attractive market town of Marlborough. A borough since 1204, it has a very wide main street lined with some fine 18th-century houses. The famous Polly Tea Rooms with its afternoon teas provides perfect post-walk refreshment.

it to be buried again to avoid publicity. George died shortly afterwards and it was thought that the mosaic had subsequently been destroyed until it was rediscovered by archaeologists in 1978. Excavations have continued over the 3 acre (1.2ha) site but you will find the showpiece of the villa, the superb Orpheus mosaic, beautifully restored and relaid in its original position. Dating from around AD 360, it plays an important role in our understanding of early Christian architecture.

Continue through the grounds of Littlecote House. The right of way soon passes in front of the house and down the avenue of trees to the gatehouse and road.

Built between 1490 and 1520, Littlecote is an exquisite manor house standing amidst spacious lawns and gardens, with the River Kennet running through the surrounding parkland. Behind the building's long, gabled façade are some fine architectural treasures, notably the 110ft (33.5m) Long Gallery, the oak-panelled Great Hall, and the magnificent Cromwellian chapel, probably the only complete example of its kind in England.

Tales of mystery, intrigue and royal visits abound at Littlecote, now an adults-only hotel. Jane Seymour is said to have entertained Henry VIII here before their marriage. Later, Charles II dined here with Colonel Alexander Popham. In 1688 William of Orange met with the commissioners of King James II at the house. Among the regular sightings of ghosts have been that of a mother and her baby, a midwife and that of Will Darrell who owned the

estate in the mid-16th century. Known as 'Wild' Darrell for his unruly lifestyle, it is said that he had many mistresses, including his own sister whom he made pregnant. One night he called for Mother Barnes, a midwife, to deliver the child. She was brought blindfolded into a secret chamber off the Long Gallery, delivered the child and gave it to Darrell who immediately threw it on the fire. Although rewarded with gold, the midwife's conscience troubled her and she finally told the local magistrate. Darrell was brought to trial, accused of murder, before Judge Popham but was aquitted after bribing Popham with the offer of Littlecote House. A year later Darrell was killed falling from his horse.

Turn right, ascend the narrow lane then, where it turns sharp left, keep straight on through gates, signed 'Ramsbury'. As the metalled track swings right, go straight ahead along the gravelled track. At a junction of tracks, fork right along a concrete track, following the bridle path uphill. Where the concrete track swings right into woodland near the top of the hill, take the path ahead just within the woodland fringe. The path soon veers right, descends into the valley and follows the left-hand edge of a field to reach the track and cottage encountered on the outward route. Retrace your steps back into Ramsbury.

WALK 5

# Clarendon's Lost Palace

*Explore ancient woodland for the remains of Clarendon Palace.*

DISTANCE 7.5 miles (12.1km)   MINIMUM TIME 3hrs

ASCENT/GRADIENT 410ft (125m) ▲▲▲   LEVEL OF DIFFICULTY ✦✦✦

PATHS Field paths, woodland tracks, country lanes, 10 stiles

LANDSCAPE Gently undulating farmland and woodland

SUGGESTED MAP OS Explorers 131 Romsey, Andover & Test Valley and 130 Salisbury & Stonehenge

START/FINISH Grid reference: SU 212312 (on Explorer 131)

DOG FRIENDLINESS Keep dogs under control across farmland

PARKING Pitton village hall. Considerate roadside parking in Pitton

PUBLIC TOILETS None on route

The parish of Pitton and Farley lies on the boundary of a vast estate, Clarendon Park, which occupies a wide arc of country due east of Salisbury. In Saxon times the area was covered with an ancient forest and within its bounds are the remains of the once magnificent Clarendon Palace, which began its life as a Saxon hunting lodge. It was expanded by the Plantagenets into a great country house becoming, in the 14th century, second only to the Palace of Westminster in size and importance.

## Royal Residence

Henry II and Henry III were both responsible for creating this grand building with its great hall, lavish apartments, council chambers and chapels, all beautifully adorned with wall-paintings and floor tiles. Many great names in history visited the palace as a place of retreat and pleasure, notably Thomas Beckett and the captive kings, John of France and David of Scotland, who hunted with their captor, King Edward III, in the surrounding forests.

The palace continued to be an occasional residence of the royal family until the outbreak of the War of the Roses in 1455. At the end of the conflict in 1485, although in decline, the palace was sustained and occasionally visited by Yorkist, Tudor and Stuart monarchs until the land and the now almost ruined building was confiscated by Parliament in the wake of the execution of Charles I in 1649.

The archaeologist Dr Tancred Borenius excavated the site during the 1930s revealing evidence of a Saxon building below Norman foundations. He also identified the great hall, the kitchens, the royal quarters and several council chambers. Until recently, very little could be seen, except for a few ruined walls and broken floors. You can now view the results of the on-going excavations that are once again beginning to reveal the hidden history and glory of this once magnificent palace.

Just south of Pitton is the village of Farley, a fragmented settlement built around a triangle of lanes with a pleasant assortment of buildings. It is known for its classical church, built of country brick in a style influenced by

# PITTON

Sir Christopher Wren. The church was built for Sir Stephen Fox who was born in the village of poor parentage, but being an able and intelligent man he served Charles II, eventually rising to the post of Paymaster General. He later contributed £13,000 (then a huge sum of money) to the building of

Chelsea Hospital and in doing so became a friend of Wren. Fox later bought Farley Manor and employed Alexander Fort, an architect who had worked with Wren, to build the handsome village church between 1689 and 1690. The interior has simple panelling and pews, a broad central aisle, some fine monuments and classical-style window glass.

## WALK 6 DIRECTIONS

**1** Locate The Silver Plough pub and walk up a cul-de sac to the right of it. In 100yds (91m), take the footpath right, heading uphill between houses to a stile. Proceed across a narrow field to a stile, then go ahead along the right-hand field-edge to a gap.

**2** Cross the track and continue along another track to the right of woodland. It narrows and soon reaches a stile. Keep ahead to enter Church Copse. Where the fenced path joins a track bear right then, at a junction on the woodland fringe, keep straight on downhill into Farley village.

**3** At the road, turn right and pass All Saints Church and the almshouses. Leave the village and take the second path on the left (the first has a coronation tree and plaque). Go diagonally right and follow the hedge right to a stile by a bungalow. Walk down the drive, cross the lane to a gate and follow the path through a long field to a stile and gate.

**4** Proceed across the next field (on the left of power cables) to a stile and gate. Take the track

immediately right and follow this byway to a track T-junction with a footpath into a field on the right. Turn left alongside a fenced enclosure and, on emerging from the wood, head straight across two fields and enter further woodland.

**5** Walk through the woodland alongside a clearing to your right, and cross a lane back into woodland. Leave the wood and follow the track right, then left around the field-edge and soon re-enter the wood. Keep ahead where the Clarendon Way merges from the right and continue to the ruins of Clarendon Palace.

**6** From the palace remains, retrace your steps through the wood, this time keeping left along the Clarendon Way. Follow the path for nearly a mile (1.6km) through the wood. On emerging, keep straight on down the track and cross the lane by a barn.

**7** Pass beside white cottages and woodland to your right, then walk down a fenced path, soon to follow the diverted footpath signs to the sewage pumping station. At the lane turn left, then right, back to the village hall.

# Amesbury and the Woodford Valley

*Catch a glimpse of Stonehenge on this downland and riverside ramble.*

| | |
|---|---|
| DISTANCE | 6.5 miles (10.4km)   MINIMUM TIME 3hrs |
| ASCENT/GRADIENT | 518ft (158m) ▲▲   LEVEL OF DIFFICULTY ✦✦✦ |
| PATHS | Tracks, field and bridle paths, roads, 2 stiles |
| LANDSCAPE | River valley and chalk downland |
| SUGGESTED MAP | OS Explorer 130 Salisbury & Stonehenge |
| START/FINISH | Grid reference: SU 149411 |
| DOG FRIENDLINESS | Keep dogs on lead through villages and water-meadows |
| PARKING | Free parking at Amesbury Recreation Ground car park |
| PUBLIC TOILETS | Amesbury |

Amesbury is a pleasant market town set in a bend of the River Avon, which is crossed by a five-arched bridge built in Palladian style. Its proximity to the eastern edge of Salisbury Plain means that the neighbourhood is dominated by large military camps, including the experimental flying base of Boscombe Down. Despite this, the lesser-known chalk downland and the beautiful Woodford Valley to the south of the town remain delightfully unspoilt. Criss-crossed by breezy byways and tranquil riverside paths, it is perfect walking country with archaeological treasures, such as Bronze Age barrows and of course Stonehenge, and chocolate-box villages.

## Amesbury Abbey

According to legend, Amesbury was founded by an uncle of King Arthur, a Roman Briton named Ambrosius Aurelianus, hence the name Amesbury. After Arthur's death in the 6th century AD, it is said that Queen Guinevere sought refuge in the Wessex region, probably retreating to Amesbury Abbey. The abbey was succeeded in AD 979 by a nunnery which eventually became the richest in England. It achieved fame as the refuge of Mary, daughter of Edward I, and her grandmother Queen Eleanor, Henry III's widow. After the Dissolution of the Monasteries in 1540, the convent was demolished and a house was built on the site. This was replaced in 1661 by a new mansion, designed by John Webb in the style of Inigo Jones, his father-in-law. Here, the handsome and hospitable Duchess of Queensberry inspired John Gay to write *The Beggar's Opera* (1728).

The present Amesbury Abbey was rebuilt in 1840 by Thomas Hopper for Sir Edward Antrobus, owner of the Stonehenge Estate. Although it is now a nursing home, you can see the colonnaded front from the impressive neoclassical entrance in Church Street. Amesbury's ancient and atmospheric church is all that remains of the original abbey. Built by the Saxons and remodelled by the Normans, it has a fine example of an early 14th-century window in the chancel, striking tracery and carved bosses.

The meandering River Avon threads its way south from Amesbury for 7 miles (11.3km), flowing through the Woodford Valley to Salisbury in the

# AMESBURY

Avon Valley. Peaceful and protected, it is the perfect setting for some of Wiltshire's finest villages, notably the three Woodfords and Great Durnford, the quintessential English village with its converted mill, weeping willows, picture-postcard thatched cottages with flower-filled gardens, impressive Norman church and handsome manor house. Take time to visit the church and, if the pub is open, relax with a pint in the garden, which overlooks the lush water-meadows.

## WALK 7 DIRECTIONS

**1** Take the footpath to the right of the play area, cross a footbridge and bear right to cross the main footbridge over the River Avon. At a crossing of tracks, take the track signed 'Durnford', passing to the right of cottages. Head uphill to a junction and go straight on, downhill to a gate. Turn right along the field-edge and bear left in the corner to join a path that passes through the valley bottom beside a stream to shortly cross a footbridge on your right.

**2** Follow the path through marshy ground to cross a bridge over the Avon. Bear right over a small bridge and keep left through a paddock beside the thatched cob wall of Normanton Down House to a stile. Bear right along the fenced path beside the drive to the road. Turn left then, in 0.25 mile (400m), reach a right turn.

❸ Either walk up the tarmac road towards Springbottom Farm or join the path through the spinney on your right for views across to Stonehenge. Pass a covered reservoir and some barns, then descend to the farm complex. Just beyond the barns, bear left with a red byway arrow on to a track beside paddocks.

❹ Keep to this track through the downland valley (Lake Bottom) for nearly one mile (1.6km). Where it becomes metalled take the arrowed path right, between new fences, into woodland and bear left uphill. Once out of the trees, keep right along the field-edge, with views left to Lake House, to a stile.

❺ Cross the lane and take the bridle path right in front of a thatched house. Go past (not through) a gap on your left, to descend gently. Cross a drive and bear left to cross two footbridges

over the Avon. Pass beside Durnford Mill and follow the drive out to the lane.

❻ Turn left and walk through Great Durnford, passing the church and drive to Great Durnford Manor, following the public road right, uphill through woodland. Descend and take the waymarked bridle path left beside Fairwood House.

❼ Ascend steeply through the edge of Ham Wood. On leaving the wood, do not curve left and down; pare right along a narrow path through scrub to a gate. Keep right along two fenced field-edges to a gate.

❽ Maintain your direction through the pastureland, not losing height, eventually easing right towards a field boundary corner. Continue for 0.25 mile (400m), following a field-edge. Keeping this line, descend the field-edge to a gate to rejoin your outward route. Retrace your steps back into Amesbury and the car park.

# Avon Valley from Downton

*Discover Downton's architectural heritage and an 18th-century estate associated with Lord Nelson.*

DISTANCE 5 miles (8km)   MINIMUM TIME 2hrs 30min

ASCENT/GRADIENT 229ft (70m) ▲▲▲   LEVEL OF DIFFICULTY ✦✦✦

PATHS Riverside paths, downland tracks, metalled lanes, 5 stiles

LANDSCAPE River valley, woodland, downland pasture, village streets

SUGGESTED MAP OS Explorers 130 Salisbury & Stonehenge;
131 Romsey, Andover & Test Valley

START/FINISH Grid reference: SU 180214 (on Explorer 130)

DOG FRIENDLINESS Keep dogs under control across pasture

PARKING Plenty of roadside parking in High Street

PUBLIC TOILETS None on route

Close to the Hampshire border and straddling the channels of the River Avon south of Salisbury, Downton has the air of a small town about it. Despite this, the central area, known as The Borough, with its wide and pretty green and thatched timber-framed cottages, has not lost its village feel. This is the medieval Downton built as a 'new town' by the Bishop of Winchester around 1205, close to The Moot, an earthwork that was once the site of a palace built in 1138 by Henry de Blois for the Bishops of Winchester. Gracing this historic plot is Moot House, an 18th-century mansion set in landscaped grounds that include an amphitheatre, lily pond and viewpoint. Near by stands the Manor House, formerly the parsonage, an Elizabethan house once owned by the Raleigh family.

Downton was made a borough in the 13th century, entitling the town to hold markets and fairs. It supported a mayor and sent two MPs to Parliament between 1395 and 1832. It was a profitable borough as burgesses paid their rents in cash rather than holding land against feudal labour and produce. Downton continued to prosper as industry and commerce flourished. Lace was produced as a cottage industry here, and the village has long been associated with flour- and paper-milling. From 1885 Wiggins Teape Carter and Barlow produced handmade paper until the end of the First World War. For centuries the village has supported thriving trout fisheries and today Downton is renowned as an angling centre for the Wiltshire Avon.

## Admiral Nelson's House

Over the River Avon, east of Charlton All Saints, is a large mansion set in parkland. Dating back to the 18th century, and once known as Standlynch House, it was acquired by the Treasury in 1814 and renamed Trafalgar House after being given to the heirs of Admiral Viscount Nelson in recognition of the services of Britain's greatest seafaring hero. The Nelson family lived here until 1948. In the redundant chapel, once the Nelson family's private chapel and now sadly boarded up, you can see the Nelson name on some of the gravestones.

WALK 8

157 ▲
Pepperbox
Hill

Brickworth Down

The Pepperbox
(Eyre's Folly)

145 ▲

Ⓟ

Ⓐ

Witherington
Down

← Salisbury

A36

Reservoir

Ⓑ

153 ▲

Dismantled Railway

Ⓒ

Barford
Down

Barford Down
Farm

❺

87 ▲

Standlynch
Lodge

Ⓓ   109 ▲

❻

Trafalgar
House

❹

Barford
Cliff

93 ▲

100 ▲

❼

Mill

Barford
Park

B3080

❸

Charlton

A338

River Avon

❷

Kings Arms

❶

Downton

† The Moot

0      ½ mile

0            1km

B3080

White Horse
Inn

Wick

Breamore House

**WALK 8**

## WALK 8 DIRECTIONS

**1** Head west along the High Street, cross the river bridge and take the metalled footpath right, signed 'Charlton All Saints'. Walk alongside the river, go through a kissing gate and keep to the footpath as it swings away from the river along a causeway through water-meadows. When the path widens and bears left, fork right to a stile and footbridge.

**2** Turn right along a concrete track then, as this bears to the left towards farm buildings, fork right through a kissing-gate and keep to the right-hand field-edge to a small brick bridge and kissing-gate. Now cross two fields to reach a kissing gate by a house. Cross the gravel drive and stile opposite. Walk beside the hedge on your right, following it left, then continue straight ahead to a public footbridge.

**3** Cross a stile and a further footbridge, and walk through reedy marshland. Pass through an old gateway and then cross a series of footbridges to reach a mill. Turn left in front of the mill and follow the concrete driveway. In 100yds (91m), take the waymarked footpath sharp left (bear right to the chapel), uphill through woodland, eventually reaching a fork.

**4** Take the main path right to a stile on the woodland edge. Bear half right across a field to a gate

(Trafalgar House is on your right), and follow the woodland path for 0.25 mile (400m) to a metalled lane. Turn right uphill, then left at the junction opposite a lodge.

**5** Cross the bridge over the disused railway and take the arrowed bridle path right (to follow Walk 9, keep to the lane here). Continue beside the old railway, following the right-hand edge of two fields to reach a road.

**6** Turn right under the bridge, then left to follow the old embankment. When this peters out, maintain direction over the hill and descend to cross the path where Walk 9 rejoins the main walk route.

**7** Descend into the valley and, as you start to ascend, take the path to the right of the embankment. At the top of the rise, turn left over a stile and continue beside the old railway. Cross a stile and keep ahead along an enclosed path to a residential road. Keep ahead for 50yds (46m) and turn right down a signposted path to a gate. Walk down the drive and turn left back to the High Street.

# Pepperbox Hill

*A more strenuous loop takes you*
*high above the Avon Valley.*
**See map and information panel for Walk 8**

---

**DISTANCE** *7.75 miles (12.5km)* **MINIMUM TIME** *4hrs*
**ASCENT/GRADIENT** *410ft (125m)* ▲▲▲ **LEVEL OF DIFFICULTY** ✚✚✚

---

## WALK 9 DIRECTIONS
## (Walk 8 Option)

Cross the bridge over the old railway, Point **5**, and keep to the lane. At the sharp right bend, take the middle of three tracks ahead of you. Fork right in 50yds (46m), go through a gate, and begin a long, steady climb up the track. Eventually, follow the wooded track downhill to the A36, Point **A**. Cross the road with extreme care and follow the byway ahead, signed 'Pepperbox Hill'. Access to the folly is via the car park on your right.

Built by Giles Eyre in 1606, The Pepperbox, or Eyre's Folly, is generally regarded as one of the earliest follies in the country. It is hexagonal and brick built, with a pyramidal roof, and the windows have been bricked in on all three levels. It is believed that Eyre was envious of the towers of nearby Longford Castle and built his tower on high ground so he could overlook the castle. Some say it is not a folly at all and that Eyre built it as a hunting viewing stand.

The 24 acre (9.7ha) site on which The Pepperbox stands is one of the finest examples of chalk grassland and scrub mosaic in the county, supporting yew woodland, hawthorn and privet thickets, and juniper. The open areas and glades attract the orange clearwing moth, brimstone and grizzled skipper butterflies, while the colourful grassland in summer supports horseshoe vetch, birdsfoot trefoil, bee orchids and wild thyme.

Retrace your steps across the main road then, at the end of the trees, fork left along a grassy track. Walk past an aerial and covered reservoir and head downhill on a gravel track beside woodland. At a T-junction, Point **B**, turn left then almost immediately right, down another track. At a fork, bear right and continue within the edge of the woodland. This soon becomes a track between fields. At the crossing of tracks, Point **C**, turn right and just before reaching a metalled lane, take the track left waymarked 'Restricted byway'. Walk past Barford Down Farm and ascend the grassy track which soon passes through woodland into a field. Keep left, pass a gate and in 75yds (69m) bear right across the brow of Barford Down, Point **D**, on an indistinct path. Descend across a bridleway and though a gap in the hedge; then, in 400yds (366m), turn left at the crossing of paths and join Walk 8 at Point **7** to return to Downton.

# Vale of Pewsey and Oare Hill

*Combine a gentle canalside stroll with a stiff downland climb to the summit of Oare Hill for magnificent views.*

WALK 10

| | |
|---|---|
| **DISTANCE** 5 miles (8km) | **MINIMUM TIME** 2hrs 15min |
| **ASCENT/GRADIENT** 393ft (120m) ▲▲▲ | **LEVEL OF DIFFICULTY** ✦✦✦ |

**PATHS** Tow paths, tracks, field paths, lanes, 2 stiles
**LANDSCAPE** Vale of Pewsey and chalk downland
**SUGGESTED MAP** OS Explorer 157 Marlborough & Savernake Forest
**START/FINISH** Grid reference: SU 157610
**DOG FRIENDLINESS** Let off lead along tow path
**PARKING** Fee-paying car park at Pewsey Wharf
**PUBLIC TOILETS** None on route

## WALK 10 DIRECTIONS

The Vale of Pewsey separates Wiltshire's two principal areas of chalk downland, Salisbury Plain to the south and the Marlborough Downs to the north. Through its heart meanders the Kennet and Avon Canal, the longest and most important of the canals within Wiltshire, built between 1794 and 1810 to link the River Kennet, which flows into the Thames at Reading, with the River Avon at Bath. It was used to carry iron, coal, stone and timber from Bristol and to bring luxuries like tobacco and spirits from London.

### WHILE YOU'RE THERE

Visit nearby Pewsey and its heritage centre in the High Street. Housed in an 1870s foundry, it contains a collection of agricultural machinery. Cut into Pewsey Hill south of the village is the Pewsey White Horse, carved in 1937 on the site of an older horse (1785) to celebrate the coronation of George VI. The climb is worth it for the inspiring views.

The canal company built the wharf at Pewsey to serve the village, but it was never a great commercial success and was eclipsed by those at nearby Burbage to the east and Honey Street to the west. It remains much as it was in the past. The main buildings consist of a cottage, which would have housed the wharfinger – owner or keeper – of the wharf, and the two-storey warehouse, used to store goods transported by canal.

Facing the canal, turn right along the tow path and walk beside the canal for just over a mile (1.6km) to the second bridge. Cross the stile on your right before the bridge and turn left along the lane, crossing the canal bridge. At a road junction, keep ahead towards downland. Pass cottages on your right and proceed ahead through the gateway along the drive. Where this bears left to West Wick House, continue straight on along the grass-centred track, which soon narrows and begins to climb steadily towards Martinsell Hill. Go through a gate, avoid a path on the immediate left

**WHAT TO LOOK OUT FOR**

From the Giant's Grave, look west across Oare to locate Oare House on the west side of the village. This small mansion has associations with Clough Williams-Ellis of Portmeirion fame. He added the symmetrical wings in the 1920s.

and bear left at the fork to ascend a steep sunken lane (note that this can be muddy).

At the top, keep left of the gate, disregard the waymarked stile on your right and bear left alongside the fence, following a path towards the long barrow on the summit of Oare Hill.

The Giant's Grave is an ancient unchambered burial site that has a charming legend associated with it. It is claimed that the giant will stir from his slumbers if anyone runs around the tomb seven times. Standing as it does on the top of Oare Hill, it is a splendid vantage point from which to savour far-reaching views across the Vale of Pewsey and the North Wessex Downs. You can also see the impressive combes and dry valleys etched into the downland scarp slopes away to your right. The unimproved chalk downlands along the steep escarpment of the vale and on nearby Martinsell Hill are noted for their extremely rich chalk grassland flora, notably cowslip, burnt orchid and devil's bit scabious, and a wide variety of butterflies including Adonis and chalkhill blue and dark green fritillary.

Follow the path past the trig point and descend the steep grassy slope towards Oare, soon to reach a stile at the bottom. Bear left along the field-edge and follow the path across the field

to a gate and crossing of ways. Take the footpath ahead, bearing right, then left around the field edge to reach a lane. Turn left and pass a bungalow. Continue on the lane and take the next track on the right, heading in a southerly direction across open farmland. Keep ahead where it bears right towards a farm and continue to the Kennet and Avon Canal. Cross the bridge and bear left back down to rejoin the tow path, passing Jones's Mill – The Vera Jeans Nature Reserve.

**WHERE TO EAT AND DRINK**

Occupying the former wharfinger's cottage and with its small canalside garden, the welcoming Waterfront Café at Pewsey Wharf offers light lunches and snacks all day and is the perfect resting place after you have completed your walk. Alternatively, try the French Horn pub across the bridge.

Bordering the River Avon and fed by numerous springs, this wetland reserve, or fen, is a rare environment within Wiltshire and an exciting place because of the diverse wildlife it supports. Since the water-meadows were abandoned, the site has developed an exceptionally rich flora with 14 species of sedge (a grass-like plant) alone. Dotted among the sedge you will also find bogbean, bog pimpernel and southern marsh orchid. An unusual sight are the belted Galloway cattle which graze the fen to keep the coarser vegetation at bay, thus allowing the more delicate flowers to thrive. The wet woodland in the middle of the reserve has an understorey of huge tussock sedges and great horsetails creating a prehistoric landscape. Retrace your steps back to the car park at Pewsey Wharf.

*Overleaf: Oare Hill (Walk 10)*

# Salisbury's Historic Trail

*A gentle urban stroll around the streets and ancient pathways of one of England's loveliest cathedral cities.*

| | |
|---|---|
| DISTANCE | 3 miles (4.8km) |
| MINIMUM TIME | 2hrs (longer if visiting attractions) |
| ASCENT/GRADIENT | Negligible ▲▲▲    LEVEL OF DIFFICULTY ✦✦✦ |
| PATHS | Pavements and metalled footpaths |
| LANDSCAPE | City streets and water-meadows |
| SUGGESTED MAP | OS Explorer 130 Salisbury & Stonehenge; AA Street by Street Salisbury |
| START/FINISH | Grid reference: SU 141303 |
| DOG FRIENDLINESS | Not suitable for dogs |
| PARKING | Central car park (signed off A36 Ring Road) |
| PUBLIC TOILETS | Central car park, Market Place, Crane Bridge Road |

Salisbury, or New Sarum, founded in 1220 following the abandonment of Old Sarum and built at the confluence of four rivers, is one of the most beautiful cathedral cities in Britain. Relatively free from sprawling suburbs and high-rise development, the surrounding countryside comes in to meet the city streets along the river valleys. Throughout the city centre, buildings of all styles blend harmoniously, from the 13th-century Bishop's Palace in The Close, the medieval gabled houses and historic inns and market places to stately pedimented Georgian houses and even the modern shopping centre.

## Majestic Cathedral and Close

Salisbury's skyline is dominated by the magnificent spire of the cathedral, a graceful centrepiece to the unified city. An architectural masterpiece, built in just 38 years during the 13th century, the cathedral is unique for its uniformity of style. The tower and spire, with a combined height of 404ft (123m) – the tallest in England – were added in 1334, and the west front of the building is lavishly decorated with row upon row of beautifully carved statues in niches. The rich and spacious interior contains huge graceful columns of Purbeck stone, and many windows add to the airy, dignified interior. Of particular interest are the impressive tombs and effigies in the nave, the cloisters and the library, home to a copy of the Magna Carta.

Originally built to house the clerics, the Cathedral Close is the one of the largest and finest in Britain. It is entered by a series of medieval gateways and contains several grand structures in a rich variety of architectural styles, dating from the 13th century to the present day. Four of these fine buildings are open to the public as museums. The highlights are probably Malmesbury House, originally a 13th-century canonry, with its magnificent roccoco plasterwork and an Orangery that once sheltered Charles II, and Mompesson House (owned by the National Trust), an exquisite Queen Anne building with period furnishings, china and paintings.

## City Streets

Beyond The Close, Salisbury is a delight to explore. You can wander through a fascinating network of medieval streets and alleys, with names like Fish Row, Silver Street and Ox Row, lined with half-timbered and jettied houses. On this city walk you will see the 15th-century St Thomas's church, noted for its *Doom* painting (c1475), believed to be the largest painting of the Last Judgment in existence, the hexagonally buttressed 15th-century Poultry Cross, the last of four market crosses in the city, the timbered medieval house of John A'Port (Crew Clothing Co) in Queen Street, and the Joiners' Hall with its superb Jacobean façade in St Ann Street.

Away from the hustle and bustle, your riverside stroll through Queen Elizabeth Gardens and along the Town Path to Harnham Mill will reveal the famous view across the water-meadows to the cathedral, much admired by many an artist.

## WALK 11 DIRECTIONS

❶ Join the Riverside Walk and follow the signposted path through the Maltings Shopping Centre towards St Thomas's church. On reaching St Thomas's Square, close to the Polly Tearooms, bear right to the junction of Bridge Street, Silver Street and the High Street.

**②** Turn left along Silver Street and cross the road to the Poultry Cross. Keep ahead along Butcher Row and Fish Row to pass the Guildhall and tourist information centre. Turn right along Queen Street and turn right along New Canal to view the cinema foyer.

**③** Return to the crossroads and continue ahead along Milford Street to pass the Red Lion. Turn right along Brown Street, then left along Trinity Street to pass Trinity Hospital. Pass Love Lane into Barnard Street and follow the road right to reach St Ann Street, opposite the Joiners' Hall.

> ### WHERE TO EAT AND DRINK
> Old pubs, tea rooms and restaurants abound around the cathedral and its close. Try the Lemon Tree in Crane Street, the Polly Tearooms in St Thomas's Square, or the historic Haunch of Venison in Minster Street. Enjoy a civilised afternoon tea in the garden of Mompesson House in The Close.

**④** Walk down St Ann Street and keep ahead on merging with Brown Street to reach the T-junction with St John's Street. Cross straight over and go through St Ann's Gate into the Cathedral Close. Pass Malmesbury House and Bishops Walk and take the path diagonally left across the green to reach the main entrance to the cathedral.

**⑤** Pass the entrance, walk beside the barrier ahead and turn right. Shortly, turn right again along

> ### WHAT TO LOOK OUT FOR
> Go into the foyer of the cinema in New Canal to view John Halle's 15th-century banqueting hall. Composer George Frideric Handel is thought to have given his first concert in England in the room above St Ann's Gate. While in the cathedral, look out for the 14th-century clock, believed to be the oldest working clock in the world.

West Walk, passing Salisbury and South Wiltshire Museum and the Military Museum. Keep ahead around Chorister Green to pass Mompesson House.

**⑥** Bear left through the gates into High Street and turn left at the crossroads along Crane Street. Cross the River Avon and turn left along the metalled path beside the river through Queen Elizabeth Gardens. Keep left by the play area and soon cross the footbridge to follow the Town Path across the water-meadows to the Old Mill (hotel) in Harnham.

**⑦** Return along Town Path, cross the footbridge and keep ahead to Crane Bridge Road. Bear right, recross the Avon and turn immediately left along the riverside path to Bridge Street. Cross straight over and follow the path ahead towards The Mill. Walk back through the Maltings Shopping Centre to the car park.

> ### WHILE YOU'RE THERE
> Discover more about Salisbury's fascinating history by visiting the award-winning Salisbury and South Wiltshire Museum, housed in the 14th-century King's House within The Close. Climb the steps up the cathedral tower for a bird's-eye view across the city and surrounding countryside.

# Lydiard Park – Swindon's Surprise

*A gentle rural ramble from a Palladian mansion
and country park on Swindon's urban fringe.*

---

**DISTANCE** 2.5 miles (4km)   **MINIMUM TIME** 1hr

**ASCENT/GRADIENT** 65ft (20m) ▲▲▲   **LEVEL OF DIFFICULTY** ✦✦✦

**PATHS** Well-defined parkland paths and tracks, one stretch of quiet road

**LANDSCAPE** Farmland, parkland, woodland

**SUGGESTED MAP** OS Explorer 169 Cirencester & Swindon

**START/FINISH** Grid reference: SU 101844

**DOG FRIENDLINESS** Can be off lead in country park

**PARKING** Free parking at Lydiard Country Park

**PUBLIC TOILETS** Lydiard Country Park

---

Right on the edge of the modern town of Swindon lies the 244-acre (99ha) Lydiard Park, an easily accessible and delightful buffer against any further westward urban spread. Within the wooded and eminently explorable park is one of Wiltshire's smaller and lesser known stately homes, a Palladian mansion, the ancestral home of the Viscounts Bolingbroke, and their church, St Mary's, in the village of Lydiard Tregoze. This walk takes you through the park to the edge of the sleepy hamlet of Hook Street, following signposted paths and tracks.

## Lydiard House and Park

The present house, built in 1743, was saved from dereliction by the Swindon Corporation in 1943. Part of the property now serves as a hostel but the ground floor has been restored to its former 19th-century glory, complete with ornate plasterwork, original family furnishings, a rare painted glass window, portraits of the St John family (the Bolingbrokes) who lived here from Elizabethan times, and lifelike waxwork inhabitants. As one of Wiltshire's smaller stately homes, it has an intimate atmosphere rarely found in larger houses that have opened their doors to the public. Here you have the impression of stepping back in time to pay a social call on wealthy relations, a family, which like many of us, has had its share of ups and downs. Even the park has had its misfortunes; it was used as a prisoner of war camp at the end of the Second World War and later lost all the fine elm trees, which lined the driveway from 1911, to Dutch elm disease.

## The Bolingbroke Family

During the Civil War the Bolingbrokes sided with the losing Royalists and although rewarded during the Restoration were disappointed when Henry St John (1652–1742) was bestowed with the title of a 'mere' Viscount in 1712 rather than becoming an Earl. Rather too close a friendship with France in the early 18th century led to a period of exile for Henry before he received a royal pardon. In 1768 the Second Viscount, Frederick St John, sensationally for the time, divorced his wife, Lady Diana Spencer, daughter of the Duke of Marlborough. Further periods of 'absenteeism', this time to Germany and heavy mortgage liabilities finally saw the break up of the estate in the 1920s and 30s.

## St Mary's Church

The church contains a further history of the family in the form of memorials. Family trees, paintings, stained-glass windows and tomb effigies are all in evidence. The most impressive of the latter is The Golden Cavalier, a magnificent, lifesize, fully gilded, statue of Sir John St John (1585–1648). He emerges from his tent fully clad for one of the Civil War battles. As imposing as he looks one cannot but think of the inner sadness of a man who in that conflict lost his King and three of his sons.

WALK 12

## WALK 12 DIRECTIONS

**1** Turn left out of the car park, pass the Forest Café and continue along the track to Lydiard House and the church. With the church on your right, bear left through the car park, ignoring the gate on your right, and go through another gate. Walk beside a walled garden and follow the path left into woodland.

# LYDIARD PARK

❷ Just before reaching a small clearing, turn right signposted Lydiard Millicent and Purton to reach a gate on the woodland edge. Proceed straight ahead across the field on a defined path to a bridge spanning a stream.

❸ Pass beneath electricity cables and turn left at a junction signposted West Park Circuit. Follow the straight path with plantations to the right and at the next junction, with a path to Lydiard Millicent on the right, turn left on the path marked West Park Circuit.

❹ Keep woodland on the right and follow a broad track. Go through gates and continue ahead, avoiding a left-hand path back to Lydiard House on the left. Keep ahead with hedgerow and trees to your right and at the first field

corner bear right to the road at Hook Street.

❺ Turn left, follow the narrow lane between fields and trees, pass under cables again and avoid a stile and footpath on the right. Turn left a few paces beyond it, through a galvanised kissing gate.

❻ Bear right, following the field edge, and make for a copse. Pass alongside it to reach a gate. Just beyond it turn left onto a grassy path running alongside wire fencing. Follow it across a long rectangular pasture and swing right with the field boundary. Merge with a clearly defined track, with Lydiard House seen ahead framed by trees. Head for the clearing and retrace your steps back to the country park and car park.

# Grovely Wood from Great Wishford

*Learn all about Wiltshire's oldest surviving custom on this peaceful walk through ancient Grovely Wood.*

---

DISTANCE *5 miles (8km)*  MINIMUM TIME *2hrs 30min*

ASCENT/GRADIENT *370ft (113m)* ▲▲▲  LEVEL OF DIFFICULTY +++

PATHS *Woodland paths and downland tracks*

LANDSCAPE *Chalk downland, wooded hillside and lush water-meadow*

SUGGESTED MAP *OS Explorer 130 Salisbury & Stonehenge*

START/FINISH *Grid reference: SU 080353*

DOG FRIENDLINESS *Can be off lead through Grovely Wood*

PARKING *Roadside parking in South Street, Great Wishford*

PUBLIC TOILETS *None on route*

---

Great Wishford is the most southerly of a series of villages in the valley of the River Wylye, which gives its name to Wilton and so to the county of Wiltshire. Our knowledge of the village pre-dates the Norman conquest (1066), the written name changing over the years from Wicheford or Witford to Willesford Magna in the mid-16th century and Wishford Magna by the early 17th century. Many of the village houses are constructed of Chilmark stone, quarried in the next valley. Some are interlaced with flint, others are thatched. many are steeply roofed and date from 1628.

### 'Grovely and All Grovely'

Mention the village of Great Wishford and most Wiltshire people will immediately associate it with one date in the calendar – 29th May. This is Oak Apple Day, when the only ancient custom still taking place in the county is enacted by the villagers. On this day, they commemorate their victory over the local landowner, the Earl of Pembroke, who in creating Wilton Park closed the east–west road, south of the River Nadder, thus interfering with their ancient rights – from a charter granted in 1603 – to cut and gather timber in the nearby Grovely Wood.

Celebrations begin at dawn when the young people of the village wake each household by banging tin pans and shouting 'Grovely, Grovely, Grovely and All Grovely'. Armed with billhooks and accompanied by traditional musicians they walk up Grovely Lane into the woods, where they cut green branches for their houses and an oak bough which is decked with ribbons and hung from the church tower. Villagers dressed in period costume and led by the parish rector then go on to Salisbury Cathedral where further celebrations, in the form of dancing on the cathedral green and a procession to the high altar, culminate in the villagers loudly proclaiming their rights and chanting 'Grovely! Grovely! and All Grovely! Unity is strength'.

### Midsummer Tithes Auction

These unusual village celebrations are not a merely modern revival of a long-lost tradition but actually seem to date back to a pagan and primitive period when tree worship was connected with May Day celebrations. In understanding how these ancient rights, customs and traditions have survived in Great Wishford it is interesting to note that the village has been in the ownership of just three families over the last seven centuries.

### Bread Stones

An unusual feature in the village are the stone inscriptions that can be found in the east wall of the churchyard. These tablets record the price of bread in the village since the Napoleonic Wars. In 1801 it was 3s 10d a gallon, in 1904 only 10d and by 1920 it had risen to 2s 8d. The 'Gall' measures are a reminder of the days when bread was sold in semi-liquid form as dough for home baking.

**WALK 13**

## WALK 13 DIRECTIONS

**1** Head along South Street to the church and turn left at the T-junction. Walk past the Royal Oak. Go under the railway bridge and immediately turn right to walk along the waymarked bridle path beside a cemetery. Ascend the track to a gate.

**2** Walk along the left-hand field-edge to a gate, continue beside trees and bear right around the top of the field making for the opening that leads into woodland. Turn almost immediately left along the woodland track, following it for some distance to a T-junction. Turn right up the metalled lane.

**3** At the first major junction, by a patch of grass, turn left and then left again to follow a track running down a broad beech avenue (First Broad Drive) along the course of a Roman road, or Lead Road, which traversed Wessex from the lead mines of the Mendips in Somerset to join other ancient routes at Old Sarum, such as the Harrow Way to Kent. You are now walking through Grovely Wood, a fine

stretch of woodland that was once a royal hunting forest and which, together with the New Forest and Cranborne Chase, formed a very significant preserve.

**4** After a mile (1.6km), at a crossing of public bridle paths, turn left and keep to the main track downhill through the woodland, ignoring all cross paths and forks. Emerge from Grovely Wood and follow the track downhill towards Great Wishford. Pass beneath the railway line to the lane. Turn left, then fork right along South Street.

# Till and Wylye Valleys

*An loop to Stapleford via downland droves and riverside paths.*
**See map and information panel for Walk 13**

---

**DISTANCE** *4.5 miles (7.2km)*  **MINIMUM TIME** *2hrs 15min*
**ASCENT/GRADIENT** *278ft (85m)* ▲▲▲  **LEVEL OF DIFFICULTY** ✚✚✚

---

## WALK 14 DIRECTIONS (Walk 13 Option)

Unlike many of the chalk downland valleys across the Salisbury Plain, the valley of the River Till is the only one with a permanent flow of water. Numerous springs high up in the heart of the plain continuously feed the little river, which rises near Tilshead and flows south to merge with the much larger River Wylye at Stapleford.

Walk to the T-junction by the church and turn right along West Street, crossing the river to the A36. Turn left, cross the road just past the pub and fork right uphill along a track. Climb through trees and continue between fields. Keep straight on over Chain Drove, by a barn, and the next crossing of byways. Pass a copse and soon take the track left, Point **A**. Follow this track as it bears sharp left, then heads downhill and veers right, eventually reaching a lane in Stapleford, Point **B**.

There are seven other Staplefords in England, for Stapleford is the name given by the Saxons to a common feature of 'a ford marked by a post or staple' which would probably serve to indicate the shallowest place in the stream. In Wiltshire it became the name of a strategic point where the ancient road from Old Sarum to Bath crosses the Till. There are four distinct parts of the village – Uppington, Church Street, Overstreet (or 'the settlement opposite') which lies clustered beside a castle mound dating from the 12th century, and Serrington beside the A36.

Turn left, then cross the B3083 on to a bridle path. Turn left along a fenced path at Seymour Cottage, cross two footbridges and soon go through a gate to the A36. Cross over, turn right, then left along the footpath before the bridge. Cross a stile, follow the right-hand field-edge to a stile and plank bridges, then cross a field and turn left alongside the River Wylye to a footbridge, Point **C**.

Keep the river to your right, crossing more stiles and footbridges. In 100yds (91m) beyond a thatched cottage, climb the stile on your right, then cross a footbridge and further stile before turning left towards farm buildings. Cross a stile and turn right up the drive to the lane and turn left back to the church and South Street.

# Sarsen Stones on Fyfield Down

WALK 15

*Explore a prehistoric landscape
on this fascinating downland ramble.*

---

**DISTANCE** *6 miles (9.7km)*   **MINIMUM TIME** *2hrs 30min*

**ASCENT/GRADIENT** *328ft (100m)* ▲▲▲   **LEVEL OF DIFFICULTY** ✚✚✚

**PATHS** *Downland tracks and field paths*

**LANDSCAPE** *Lofty downland pasture and gallops*

**SUGGESTED MAP** *OS Explorer 157 Marlborough & Savernake Forest*

**START/FINISH** *Grid reference: SU 159699*

**DOG FRIENDLINESS** *Can be off lead along Ridgeway path*

**PARKING** *Car park close to Manton House Estate (right off A4, signed Manton, west of Marlborough)*

**PUBLIC TOILETS** *None on route*

---

## WALK 15 DIRECTIONS

Leave the car park by the track in the top right-hand corner, signposted 'White Horse Trail to Avebury and Hackpen'. Follow the track right and shortly fork left, continuing between high hedges (private roads right), then on between the gallops across Clatford Down with good views. On reaching a T-junction by a covered reservoir, turn left along the Herepath (Green Street).

The Herepath is an ancient east–west route across the Marlborough Downs. The name is derived from the Old English word 'here' meaning an army or multitude. It suggests that this may have been one of the defensive routes established by King Alfred in the 9th century AD in his struggle with the Danes.

Shortly, turn right through a gate waymarked 'Hackpen', to join a grassy track alongside a conifer plantation, then head across pasture to a gate into woodland. Follow the track (can be muddy) through the sparse woodland then, on leaving the wood, keep straight on along the right-hand field-edge. Turn left and keep parallel to a track leading to gates. Avoid them and keep ahead on a grassy track, crossing gallops to reach the Ridgeway. This ancient highway incorporates a complicated network of green lanes, and follows a natural route on high ground. It was used as a drove road or trading route and a convenient means for invaders, peaceful or warlike, to penetrate the heartland of southern England before Anglo-Saxon times. The Ridgeway National Trail forms

### WHERE TO EAT AND DRINK

There are no refreshment places along the route of this walk but, if you bring your own, the Ridgeway track with its far-reaching views provides the perfect picnic spot. Nearby Manton and Lockeridge have pubs, while Marlborough offers the full range of refreshment facilities.

only part of the route, although by linking several trails you can walk the entire route.

Turn left along the rutted and often muddy track for 0.75 mile (1.2km). At the crossways by an information board, turn left to go through a gate and on to Fyfield Down.

A feature of Fyfield Down and neighbouring Overton Down are the sarsen stones that litter this intriguing chalk limestone landscape. Sarsens are natural deposits of extremely hard siliceous sandstone that derive from Tertiary deposits, later eroded and moved by glaciation some 25 million years ago. Although found elsewhere, they are not on the scale seen in the Marlborough district. Sarsens are also known as 'druid stones' or 'grey wethers', the latter due to their resemblance at a distance to a flock of sheep, the word 'wether' coming from the Old English for sheep.

> **WHILE YOU'RE THERE**
> Visit Avebury (see Walks 18 and 19) to view the largest stone circle in Europe and explore the Alexander Keiller Museum to learn more about the prehistoric archaeology of this area.

Sarsens have been of great importance to humans since prehistoric times. The hard flints were used to make hand axes and other useful tools during the Bronze Age. From the 5th century AD to the mid-19th century, sarsens were used for building stone, constructing the nearby villages of West Overton and Lockeridge, gateposts, and as paving stones and tramway setts. More importantly, Fyfield Down was the stone quarry supplying Avebury stone circle and possibly Stonehenge. Stones weighing as much as 40 tons were dug up, sometimes shaped, and dragged over the downs by hundreds of people pulling them on wooden rollers with woven grass ropes.

In 1956 Fyfield Down was declared a National Nature Reserve, not only to protect this fine stretch of natural downland and Britain's best assemblage of sarsen stones, which support nationally important lichens, but also to preserve the extensive prehistoric field systems that exist here. As you stride across this rock-strewn landscape, note the chequerboard appearance of the field systems. Banks or 'lynchets' some 8ft (2.4m) high have formed where sarsens had been moved to create field boundaries, arresting soil movement caused by ploughing over the centuries.

Proceed along a grassy track and cross a gallop via three gates. This is prime racehorse-training country and there are many racing stables in the area. Continue to the right of a wood, then in the valley bottom, fork right off the gravel track and ascend a grassy track, passing more sarsen stones. At the top, go through the two gates that cut the corner of a wooded enclosure and turn right along the field-edge. Pass through a gate in the bottom corner, cross a gallop and continue straight on across grassland on a defined path. Cross another gallop, then follow the path over a further gallop to a furlong pole at the end of a line of trees. Swing left over yet more gallops to a waymarker post, then turn left to cross more gallops to reach a track. Turn right and follow the outward route back to the car park.

# Visiting the Historic Old Sarum

*Explore the Avon Valley and fortified Old Sarum.*

---

DISTANCE *6 miles (9.7km)*   MINIMUM TIME *2hrs*

ASCENT/GRADIENT *557ft (170m)* ▲▲▲   LEVEL OF DIFFICULTY ✚✚✚

PATHS *Footpaths, tracks, bridle paths, stretches of road, 10 stiles*

LANDSCAPE *Downland, river valley, castle rampart*

SUGGESTED MAP *OS Explorer 130 Salisbury & Stonehenge*

START/FINISH *Grid reference: SU 139326*

DOG FRIENDLINESS *Keep dogs on lead at all times*

PARKING *English Heritage car park (closes 6pm; 4pm winter)*

PUBLIC TOILETS *Old Sarum car park*

---

Set on a bleak hill overlooking modern-day Salisbury (New Sarum) stand the massive, deserted ramparts and earthworks of the original settlement of Old Sarum. People have lived on this windswept hilltop for some 5,000 years – the outer banks and ditches were constructed during the Iron Age to create a huge hill-fort. It was later inhabited by the Romans and several Roman roads converge on the site. The Saxons followed and developed a town within the prehistoric ramparts.

## The Rise of Christianity

Soon after the Conquest, the Norman invaders realised the camp's strength and built the inner earthworks. Within the massive hilltop defences they built a royal castle, two palaces, and in 1075, Bishop Osmund constructed the first cathedral. The imposition of Norman rule had a profound effect on English society, in particular upon the Church, remodelling its structure, giving a new impetus to the building or reconstruction of parish churches and encouraging the development of new monasteries and other religious institutions. Nowhere is this more evident than at Old Sarum.

Osmund's cathedral set new standards which were widely adopted in other English cathedrals. Instead of being run on monastic lines, it was served by 36 canons living in separate lodgings under the direction of four officers. The architecture was Romanesque and characterised by its lavish scale. Following Osmund's death in 1099, Bishop Roger was responsible for the ambitious rebuilding of the cathedral soon after 1100.

Old Sarum rapidly developed and for 150 years it was a thriving medieval city. As the cathedral grew more powerful, friction developed between the clergy and the military governor of the castle at Old Sarum. After Roger's death in 1139, the city went into decline and quarrelling increased between the two powers. The vitality and wealth of the Church, combined with the exposed site, lack of space to expand the cathedral and the shortage of water at Old Sarum, led to the removal of the cathedral to a new city by the River Avon in the early 13th century. Building work on the new cathedral began in 1220 and was largely completed by 1250.

# OLD SARUM

The castle remained in use until Tudor times and was one of the most notorious rotten boroughs in the country when in 1832, only ten voters returned two Members of Parliament; one was William Pitt the Elder, Prime Minister from 1766 to 1768. Today, it is deserted and you can roam across the 56 acres (22.6ha) of ramparts and ruins, admiring the Avon Valley views. A fee is charged to view the inner bailey ruins.

## WALK 16 DIRECTIONS

❶ From the car park, walk down the access road through the outer bank of the fortified site. Bear left; then, as the road bends right, go through the two gates leading to a waymarked and fenced bridle path and follow this until you reach a road.

**2** Go through the gate opposite and follow the track ahead. Pass a cottage (Shepherds Corner) and ascend the track. In 0.25 mile (400m), descend to Keeper's Cottage and a crossing of paths.

**3** Keep straight on, heading uphill and between fields into a wooded area. At a crossing of bridle paths, turn left and descend a tree-lined path. At a boundary marker, bear right and continue to a road.

**4** Turn left, then right in 50yds (46m) down a metalled lane. Cross the River Avon and two further footbridges, then follow the metalled path and drive to a road. Turn left for The Wheatsheaf Inn; otherwise, turn right and in 50yds (46m) turn left up a lane.

**5** Just before cottages and barns, turn left over a stile and walk down the left-hand field-edge, crossing two more stiles and fields. Maintain direction across the next field, cross a track and go through the hedge ahead, then in 100yds (91m) reach a road.

**6** Cross the road diagonally and take the path down a wooded track. Pass to the left of 'The Bays' to a stile and turn right between the stream and fence. Cross double stiles in the corner and turn sharp left over a stile and turn right beside the stream to a white gate and a metalled drive. Turn left and skirt Home Farm and Little Durnford Manor to a gate and road.

**7** Turn right and follow the road for 0.75 mile (1.2km) to a staggered crossroads. Keep ahead towards Salisbury, crossing the stile on your left in 100yds (91m). Bear half-left across the field, then skirt the churchyard to reach a stile, a metalled path and a further stile. Head down the next field, cross a stile and pass a barn, then cross a stile on to a fenced track.

**8** Turn left uphill towards the tree-covered ramparts. Keep left at the junction of paths by a gate, then fork right through a gate and climb on to the outer rampart. Turn right and follow the path to a gate and Old Sarum's access road. Turn left back to the car park.

ALTON BARNES

# Pewsey Vale and Down

*A varied ramble across chalk downland, rich in archaeological and natural treasures, and beside the Kennet and Avon Canal.*

| | |
|---|---|
| DISTANCE 10 miles (16.1km) | MINIMUM TIME 4 hrs |
| ASCENT/GRADIENT 492ft (150m) ▲▲▲ | LEVEL OF DIFFICULTY +++ |

PATHS Tracks, field paths, tow path, metalled lanes, 4 stiles

LANDSCAPE High downland pasture, Vale of Pewsey, village streets

SUGGESTED MAP OS Explorer 157 Marlborough & Savernake Forest

START/FINISH Grid reference: SU 115637

DOG FRIENDLINESS Keep dogs under control across downland pasture

PARKING Tan Hill car park

PUBLIC TOILETS None on route

No one who travels in Wiltshire can fail to be impressed by the sweep of softly rounded chalk downland that rises to over 800ft (244m) above the fertile farmlands of the Vale of Pewsey. Walking across such high ground is one of the greatest walking experiences in the county. Not only are the views some of the best in Wiltshire, the land is rich in ancient settlements, frontier lines and burial sites. This walk is varied and exhilarating, encapsulating these archaeological treasures as well as exploring the vale with its meandering canal and unspoilt villages. It is a tale of travelling and travellers, a preoccupation we have had since the dawn of time, travelling for sustenance, for conquest, for trade and for pleasure.

## Walking Wansdyke

The high and relatively unforested downland ridges were the prehistoric motorways. They also became the boundaries between clans and kingdoms. For the defence of one in post-Roman times, the massive bank and ditch of the Wansdyke was built, clearly visible for 12 miles (19.3km) in Wiltshire from Morgan Hill to Savernake Forest. At least two major Saxon battles were fought along its length, one in AD 592 by the neolithic long barrow now known as Adam's Grave, the best sited long barrow in Wiltshire. In more peaceful times the Wansdyke became a natural road for drovers bringing their animals to the great stock fairs at Tan Hill, echoing not only the tramp of herdsmen, but the cows and sheep that were often shod for the long trek.

Saxon settlers would have been attracted by the springs and pastureland in the valley and villages would have been established, although the twin villages of Alton Barnes and Alton Priors seem scarcely large enough to make one village. Nonetheless, each had its own church, linked by an interesting sarsen stone footpath. Next upon the scene were the navvies and bargees when the Kennet and Avon Canal was built between 1794 and 1810, providing an important link between Bristol and London. Unfortunately for the canal and its total of 107 locks, the benefits were short lived when Brunel's railway from London to Bristol opened in 1841.

53

**WALK 17**

## Alton Barnes White Horse

Spiritual as well as physical journeys also figure in this landscape. High on the downs in tumuli and barrows lie ancient chieftains, with our nearer ancestors in homely churchyards. Wiltshire is famous for the chalk figures in honour of the horse, our long-valued travelling companion. However the one etched into Milk Hill above Alton Barnes is relatively recent. Created in 1812, it measures 166ft (50.5m) high by 160ft (49m) long and is noted for the fact that the journeyman artist absconded with the £20 fee before completing the task. He was subsequently caught and hung for his crime! No perpetrators have yet suffered that fate for the crop circles, which now regularly decorate the great sweeping fields of corn around Alton Barnes. Hints of yet further journeys to come?

## WALK 17 DIRECTIONS

❶ From the car park, cross the road to a gate and follow the grassy track along the left-hand field-edge to a stile and gate. Ascend to further stile and gate, continue uphill and soon descend through earthworks to a T-junction with the Wansdyke.

❷ Turn left and continue with earthworks on your left. Begin to descend, cross a wooden barrier, then go through a gate and bear left off the Wansdyke on to a metalled track. Just after the track becomes concrete, fork right through a gate and follow the grassy track downhill to a stile and gate.

❸ Rejoin the main track by a barn. Pass more barns and continue down to the road. Avoid the road opposite. Turn left and take the next right turning for Stanton St Bernard. After the road bends left, take a path on the right between fences. Turn left at the junction to follow a metalled lane. At the T-junction, turn right and pass the church, then swing left to Pewsey Vale Riding School. Turn left here and follow the track to the Kennet and Avon Canal.

❹ Cross the canal and bear right through a gate to join the tow path. With the canal on your left, keep to the tow path for 1 mile (1.6km), passing the Barge Inn, and bear left up to the road at Honeystreet. Turn left over the bridge into Alton Barnes. In 100yds (91m), turn right, signed to St Mary's Church.

❺ Just before the church, turn left through a turnstile and walk down a cobbled path. Follow the path right, cross two footbridges via turnstiles then, where the path turns sharp right to All Saints Church in Alton Priors, turn left across the field to a kissing gate. A wall topped with thatch stands to the right.

❻ Turn left then, just beyond the village sign, take the footpath right up the right-hand edge of the field. When the path bends sharp left by trees, follow it towards a waymark. At the road, ascend it and fork left up a track to a gate leading on to Pewsey Down.

❼ Follow the track ahead, parallel to the road, and gradually it sweeps to the left, heading for windswept downland. Avoid a path running in from the left and continue along the top of the White Horse.

❽ Continue ahead on the White Horse Trail and follow it as it bends right by clumps of trees. Keep right with fields on the right and a sweeping downland combe to the left and make for the Wansdyke. Turn right and retrace your steps to the car park.

# Avebury – Pagan Pastures

*Explore the famous stone circle*
*and some fine prehistoric monuments.*

WALK 18

---

DISTANCE *5 miles (8km)*   MINIMUM TIME *2hrs 30min*

ASCENT/GRADIENT *262ft (80m)* ▲▲▲   LEVEL OF DIFFICULTY ✦✦✦

PATHS *Tracks, field paths, some road walking, 4 stiles*

LANDSCAPE *Downland pasture, water-meadows, woodland and village*

SUGGESTED MAP *OS Explorer 157 Marlborough & Savernake Forest*

START/FINISH *Grid reference: SU 099696*

DOG FRIENDLINESS *Keep dogs under control across pasture and NT property*

PARKING *Large National Trust car park in Avebury*

PUBLIC TOILETS *Avebury*

---

Avebury's great stone circle is one of the most important megalithic monuments in Europe and it shares its setting with a pretty village. The 200 stones (only 27 remain) were enclosed in a massive earthen rampart nearly a mile (1.6km) in circumference. One can only wonder at the skill, vision and beliefs, not to mention the sheer dogged hard work, that enabled the peoples of that time to move huge stones for many miles and dig thousands of tons of earth to create such landscapes.

### Alexander Keiller's Vision

Avebury today owes as much to archaeologist Alexander Keiller as to the vision of our ancient ancestors. As heir to a fortune made from marmalade, Keiller was able to indulge in his passion for archaeology. In the early 1930s he came to Avebury, which then had a thriving community within and around the 4,500-year-old circle, and determined to restore it to its original glory; a prehistoric complex on a scale to match any in the country.

All his energies and a large part of his fortune was spent on purchasing the land, excavating the stones, and although contentious to modern archaeologists, he re-erected fallen stones and set up concrete markers to replace those he believed were missing. Trees were cleared from the ditches and, as and when the opportunity arose, buildings within the circle were purchased and demolished. Some of the villagers left the area and others went to the new houses in nearby Avebury Truslow.

Keiller's work was curtailed by lack of funds and, after the Second World War, he sold the site to the National Trust. His full dreams were never realised and questions were raised as to whether he should have tried to restore the site. Should ancient landscapes be protected by riding roughshod over the interests of those who have subsequently come to live and work there? Whatever your views, there is much to see and enjoy on this walk.

Unlike at Stonehenge, you can roam freely around Avebury and this enthralling walk lets you explore some of Britain's finest prehistoric monuments. There is an imposing 1.5 mile (2.4km) avenue of standing stones from where, perhaps, ancient processions would lead down to

Swindon

Winterbourne
Monkton

C Windmill
Hill
Earthworks
▲196
Tumuli    Tumuli

B

D

Avebury
Manor

A    Hunters
House

A4

A361

A4361    P 1
Avebury
176

Beckhampton

R Kennet

191
▲
Waden
Hill

Silbury
Hill
187
▲

2   A4

West
Kennett

3

West Kennett
Long Barrow
183
▲

4

East
Kennett

Red Lion
Inn

6
Manor    WESSEX
Farm    RIDGEWAY

● Stone Circle
(Remains of)

B4003

Tumulus

202
▲
Tumuli

Tumuli

RIDGEWAY

Tumuli

5   Tumuli

● The
Sanctuary

A4

0                ½ mile
0                1km

Silbury Hill, an entirely artificial structure 130ft (40m) high. Smaller in scale but just as intriguing is the West Kennett Long Barrow, the second largest barrow in Britain at 300ft (91m) in length. There is a liberal scattering of tumuli over the area, the last resting places of many a noble and priest. Finally, alongside the A4, is The Sanctuary, the site of major wooden buildings, possibly used for religious and burial rites.

## WALK 18 DIRECTIONS

❶ From the car park, walk to the main road and turn right. In 50yds (46m), cross and go through a gate with a blue bridleway sign. Pass through another gate and follow the path alongside the river. Go through two more gates and cross two stiles, passing Silbury Hill.

❷ Beyond a gate, walk down the right-hand field-edge to a gate and the A4. Cross over and turn left, then almost immediately right through a gate. Walk down the gravel track and cross a bridge over a stream. The track soon narrows to a footpath. Go through a kissing gate and turn sharp left.

### WHILE YOU'RE THERE

To learn more about Keiller, visit the Alexander Keiller Museum which displays many of the exciting finds from his archaeological excavations in the area.

❸ To visit West Kennett Long Barrow, shortly turn right. Otherwise go straight on around the left-hand field-edge to a stile and continue along a track. At a staggered junction, keep ahead across a stile and walk along the right-hand field boundary. Keep to the right in the corner by a redundant stile and cross the stile on your right in the next corner and proceed up a narrow footpath.

❹ At a T-junction, go left and descend to the road. Turn left, then just beyond the bridge, take the bridle path sharp right. Follow the right-hand field-edge to a gap in the corner and turn sharp left following a track uphill. At the top you'll see tumuli on the right and The Sanctuary on the left. Continue to the A4.

### WHAT TO LOOK OUT FOR

Locate the huge Druid Stone, the Swindon Stone and the Barber Stone, and marvel at how they were transported and why they stay upright.

❺ Cross the A4 and head up the Ridgeway. After 500yds (457m), turn left off the Ridgeway onto a byway. Bear half right by the clump of trees on a tumuli and keep to the established track, eventually reaching a T-junction by a series of farm buildings, Manor Farm.

### WHERE TO EAT AND DRINK

Try the thatched Red Lion Inn at the heart of the stone circle for traditional pub food and atmosphere. Circle Restaurant off the High Street serves good home-made vegetarian, mostly organic food and cream teas.

❻ Turn left, signed 'Avebury', and follow the metalled track through the earthwork and straight over the staggered crossroads by the Red Lion Inn. Turn left opposite the National Trust signpost and walk back to the car park.

# Avebury and Windmill Hill

*A slightly shorter loop to the largest neolithic enclosure in Britain.*
**See map and information panel for Walk 18**

---

**DISTANCE** *4.5 miles (7.2km)*  **MINIMUM TIME** *2hrs 15min*
**ASCENT/GRADIENT** *131ft (40m)* ▲▲▲  **LEVEL OF DIFFICULTY** +++

---

## WALK 19 DIRECTIONS
## (Walk 18 Option)

Leave the car park by the path signposted to the museum, shop and restaurant. At the road, turn left, walk past the church and go right opposite the vicarage. Turn left at Hunters House, walk down the drive. Tucked away behind the church, is Avebury Manor. Originally a monastery, the present building dates from the early 16th century. Some of the rooms are open to the public. Outside the Manor, don't miss the exquisite flower and topiary gardens.

Cross a footbridge and a further bridge before forking right. In 50yds (46m), climb the stile on your right, Point **A**, and proceed ahead to cross a footbridge via stiles. Bear left across the field to a stile, head straight across the next field to double stiles then maintain direction across the following large field. Negotiate three stiles at the field boundary and follow the left-hand edge of a water-meadow to a stile, Point **B**. Turn left through a gate and ascend along the right-hand field-edge to a gate. Continue uphill to a gate on to Windmill Hill, Point **C**.

Enclosing about 21 acres (8.5ha), Windmill Hill is one of Britain's largest neolithic causeway

enclosures, consisting of three concentric ditches overlying an earlier settlement. It was a seasonal gathering place for the settlers in the Marlborough Downs area in about 3300 BC. Between the inner ditches you can see a bowl barrow and a bell barrow, which form part of a small Bronze Age burial site of about 1700–1400 BC.

Walk through the earthworks, bear half right beyond the two tumuli at the summit and keep to the right of a small wood. Go downhill to a gate. Turn left along the track, then fork right at the end of woodland into more open countryside. Follow the path to the left of woodland and go through the gate on the left. Follow the left field-edge, go through a gate on your left and continue along the right edge of the adjacent field. Cross a stile, maintain direction to a gate and along a fenced track. Bear sharp right, through a gate and turn left at a junction with a track, Point **D**.

This track becomes Bray Street, narrows to a footpath and rejoins the outward journey by the footbridges. Retrace your steps back to the car park.

# A Visit to Barbury Castle

*Explore a hill-fort and enjoy the views
on this downland ramble.*

| | |
|---|---|
| **DISTANCE** 4 miles (6.4km) | **MINIMUM TIME** 2hrs |
| **ASCENT/GRADIENT** 262ft (80m) ▲▲▲ | **LEVEL OF DIFFICULTY** ✦✦✦ |

**PATHS** Tracks and byways, field paths, metalled lanes, 3 stiles

**LANDSCAPE** Chalk downland

**SUGGESTED MAP** OS Explorer 169 Cirencester & Swindon

**START/FINISH** Grid reference: SU 156760

**DOG FRIENDLINESS** Let off lead in country park

**PARKING** Free parking at Barbury Castle Country Park

**PUBLIC TOILETS** Barbury Castle Country Park

## WALK 20 DIRECTIONS

Some of the finest scenery in southern England can be found on the chalk downlands of Wiltshire, in particular the Marlborough Downs, which extend south from Swindon across the Vale of Pewsey to the northern flanks of Salisbury Plain. These expansive landscapes, with their wide skies and smooth ridges interspersed with long shallow combes, have captured the imagination of many writers. Richard Jefferies' lyrical prose was deeply influenced by the vast open downland and the far-reaching views. His favoured spot along the northern ridge of the Marlborough Downs was on Barbury Down with its breathtaking views across the Vale of the White Horse to the Cotswolds. About 150 acres (61ha) of open land on Barbury Down have now been designated a country park.

The archaeology of the area is renowned, with a mass of ancient field monuments, including stone circles, post-Roman earthworks, field systems, burial mounds and hill-forts, littering the landscape. During the Iron Age, a succession of tribes invaded Britain, many of them settling on the North Wessex Downs where they constructed dramatic hill-forts on the downland escarpments, away from the threat of advancing enemies. One of the best known hill-forts in southern England provides the focal point of the country park and our walk.

Barbury Castle is a well-defined oval of about 12 acres (5ha), with entrances at the eastern and western sides passing through towering double ramparts, as well as ditches and other defences, which may have been added when it was re-fortified in the Saxon period. Finds from the site suggest that it was used over a long period

# BARBURY CASTLE

of time and include flint axes, Iron Age and Roman pottery, weapons, tools and jewellery. You can see many of these on display in Devizes Museum. Half a mile (800m) north of the castle lies the battlefield of Beranburth where Saxon chief Cynric and his son Ceawlin defeated the Britons in a bloody massacre. It established the Saxons as overlords of southern England and later, in AD 560, Ceawlin became King of Wessex.

Go to the far end of the car park, beyond the viewing point to a gate. Continue along the Ridgeway to the eastern entrance and enter the hill-fort. Walk around the rampart or straight across the centre to leave via the western entrance. Turn right down a lane and in 50yds (46m), turn right at the crossing of ways and walk along the gravel track 'Ridgeway Route for Vehicles'.

Used for over 4,000 years, the Ridgeway linked East Anglia with the Dorset coast. The official long-distance trail begins at Ivinghoe Beacon in Buckinghamshire and follows the chalk ridges to Avebury 85 miles (137km) away.

At the T-Junction, turn right up the metalled lane and in 250yds (229m), turn left along the waymarked bridleway. Head across the field in the direction of the aerial on the horizon. Cross into the next field to the left

of a clump of trees, keep right, following the field-edge, and pass Barbury Shooting School to reach a waymark in the field corner. Swing right towards the gap in a line of trees on the brow of the hill. At the crest bear left with the 'Millennium Trail Bridleway' waymark. At the angled junction, turn sharp right, signposted 'Millennium Trail Byway', to a stile and gate.

Steeply ascend Burderop Down to a stile and gate and continue to climb along the left-hand edge of a large field, past a memorial stone to Alfred Williams and Richard Jeffries on your right. Writer and journalist Richard Jefferies (1848–87), who was born at Coate near Swindon, is perhaps Wiltshire's best-known country writer. He spent much of his time walking the Wiltshire Downs and wrote: 'They only know a country who are acquainted with its footpaths. By the roads, indeed, the outside may be seen; but the footpaths go through the heart of the land'. His plaque on the stone faces his birthplace. On the other side of the memorial stone is a plaque for Alfred Williams (1877–1930), self-taught scholar, linguist and nature poet who was born at nearby South Marston.

Eventually reach a stile and turn left up the lane. Shortly, turn right back into the car park, or keep straight on for the shop and café.

# The Infant Thames at Cricklade

*An easy ramble across water-meadows beside the Thames and disused canals.*

DISTANCE *5.5 miles (8.8km)*  MINIMUM TIME *2hrs 30min*

ASCENT/GRADIENT *Negligible* ▲▲▲  LEVEL OF DIFFICULTY ✦✦✦

PATHS *Field paths and bridle paths, disused railway, town streets, 6 stiles*

LANDSCAPE *Flat river valley*

SUGGESTED MAP *OS Explorer 169 Cirencester & Swindon*

START/FINISH *Grid reference: SU 100934*

DOG FRIENDLINESS *Dogs can be off lead along old railway line*

PARKING *Cricklade Town Hall car park (free)*

PUBLIC TOILETS *Cricklade High Street*

The River Thames begins life in a peaceful Gloucestershire field near Cirencester. Before long it graduates to a sizeable stream, also known as the Isis at this point, on its way to the Cotswold Water Park, a vast network of lakes and pools, before reaching Cricklade, Wiltshire's northernmost town and the only one situated on the river.

Although merely a meandering willow-fringed stream as it passes through the town, research in the 19th century revealed that the river at Cricklade had been navigable by large barges during the 17th and 18th centuries. In 1607 the Burcot Commission was established for the purpose of improving the Thames as a navigable waterway from Clifton Hampden to Cricklade. With the completion of the Thames and Severn Canal in 1789 river traffic was transferred to the canal and the upper reaches of the Thames gradually became overgrown.

## Cricklade – Roman Military Post

Cricklade's advantageous position at the junction of four ancient roads may well be why it was established as the head of the navigable Thames. However, Cricklade's importance as a settlement began in Roman times when it was a significant military post on Ermine Street, the Roman road linking Cirencester and Silchester. Evidence of Roman occupation has been found in and around the town, with villas to the north and south-east. The later fortified Saxon town was built as a defence against the Danes and had its own mint. Today, the High Street has worthy buildings from the 17th and 18th centuries and two contrasting parish churches. You should not miss St Sampson's, characterised by its cathedral-like turreted tower that rises high above the town and dominates the surrounding water-meadows.

## Abandoned Communication Lines

This walk follows the River Thames north, away from Cricklade, via the Thames Path. Beyond North Meadow, your route passes beside a shallow ditch that was once the North Wilts Canal, which opened in 1819 and ran the 9 miles (14.5km) between Swindon and Latton, linking the Wilts and Berks Canal with the Thames and Severn Canal. Soon you will follow the old tow path beside the muddy, weed-clogged ditch that was once the Thames and Severn Canal, opened in 1789 to link the River Severn with the Thames at Lechlade. The canal closed to all traffic in 1927, and was finally abandoned in 1933. Later the walk heads south along a disused railway line, part of the Midland and South West Railway which was closed to passengers in 1961. Although a pleasing reminder of the railway era, the ever-present drone of traffic from the A419 across the water-meadows keeps the mind firmly in the 21st century.

## WALK 21 DIRECTIONS

❶ Turn right out of the car park, keep ahead at the roundabout and walk along the High Street. Pass St Mary's Church, then turn left along North Wall before the river bridge. Shortly, bear right to a gate and join the attractive Thames Path. Continue on this route, walking along the field-edge to reach houses.

## WHERE TO EAT AND DRINK

You will find various pubs and hotels, notably The Red Lion near the Thames, and a traditional café in Cricklade. At the halfway point on the walk, at Cerney Wick, the family-owned Crown offers traditional home-cooked food, real ales and a large garden.

❷ Go through the kissing gate on your right and bear left across the field to a gate. Follow the fenced footpath, cross a plank bridge and pass through the gate immediately on your right-hand side. Cross the river bridge and turn left through a gate. Walk beside the infant River Thames, crossing two gates to enter North Meadow.

❸ Continue and cross a stile by a bridge. Go through the gate immediately right and keep straight ahead, ignoring the Thames Path, left. Follow the path beside the disused canal. Cross a footbridge and a stile then, at a fence, bear right to cross a footbridge close to a house named The Basin. Bear right along the drive.

❹ Cross a bridge and turn left through the gateway. Shortly, bear right to join the path along the left side of the old canal. Keep to the path for 0.5 mile (800m) to the road. Turn left into Cerney Wick to reach a T-junction.

❺ Cross the stone stile opposite and keep ahead through the paddock to a stone stile and lane. Cross the lane and go through the gate opposite, continuing ahead to a kissing gate and stile. Follow the path ahead. Bear right, then left and bear off left (yellow arrow) into trees.

❻ Cross a footbridge and proceed ahead along the field-edge to a stile. Turn left along the old railway, signed 'Cricklade'. Cross the River Thames in a mile (1.6km) and keep to the path along the former trackbed to reach a bridge.

## WHILE YOU'RE THERE

Visit Cricklade's small local museum where displays illustrate the history of the town from the Roman era to the present day. Head for the attractive village of Ashton Keynes and the heart of the Cotswold Water Park, Britain's largest water park, with 133 lakes providing water sports, nature trails and a visitor centre at Keynes Country Park.

❼ Follow the gravel path to the Leisure Centre. Bear left on to the road, following it right, then turn left opposite the entrance to the Leisure Centre car park. Turn right, then next left and follow the road to the church (St Sampsons).

❽ Walk beside the barrier and turn right in front of The Gatehouse into the churchyard. Bear left to the main gates and follow the lane to a T-junction. Turn right to make your way back to the car park.

## WHAT TO LOOK OUT FOR

Walk across North Meadow, a National Nature Reserve, in spring to see many rare plants and flowers, including Britain's largest area of rare snakeshead fritillaries. At Cerney Wick, note the restored lock and the well-preserved roundhouse, originally the home of the lengthsman whose job was to look after the canal, ensuring that the level of water did not drop below the necessary minimum. In Cricklade, look for the Victorian Jubilee Clock in the High Street and the medieval carved crosses in both churchyards.

# Dinton and the Nadder Valley

*Enjoy the varied scenery, the architecture and the history of two delightful villages as you explore the unspoilt Nadder Valley.*

---

**DISTANCE** 5.25 miles (8.4km)  **MINIMUM TIME** 2hrs 30min

**ASCENT/GRADIENT** 360ft (110m) ▲▲▲  **LEVEL OF DIFFICULTY** ✦✦✧

**PATHS** Tracks, field and woodland paths, parkland, 13 stiles

**LANDSCAPE** River valley and wooded hillside

**SUGGESTED MAP** OS Explorer 130 Salisbury & Stonehenge

**START/FINISH** Grid reference: SU 009315

**DOG FRIENDLINESS** Dogs can be off lead in Dinton Park

**PARKING** Dinton Park National Trust car park

**PUBLIC TOILETS** None on route

---

The Nadder Valley is quite unlike any of the other river valleys that radiate out from Salisbury, for it is not a distinct deep valley incised in the chalk strata as is evident in the neighbouring Ebble and Wylye river valleys. This anomalous character is due to the fact that the Nadder traverses a sequence of rock types, resulting in a landscape of scarp slopes and deep combes within its broad vale. In this well-watered valley, villages free from the need to be located on the banks of the Nadder, are found scattered across the landscape, nestling among lush meadows, wooded hills and along gentle tributary streams. Your walk explores the heart of the Nadder Valley, its wooded slopes and two unspoilt villages, delightful Dinton and the charmingly named Compton Chamberlayne.

## Dinton's Famous Families

The village of Dinton, built on a hillside north of the Nadder, is bordered by three beautifully landscaped houses, each associated with important Wiltshire families. Surprisingly for such a small village, the National Trust owns four properties here – Hyde's House, Lawes Cottage, Little Clarendon and Philipps House – the latter two are open to the public during the summer months. In the old part of the village, close to St Mary's Church, you will find Hyde's House, an elegant building with a Queen Anne façade masking 16th-century origins. It was here that Charles II's chancellor, Edward Hyde was born in 1609.

His daughter Anne married the future James II and was mother to Queen Anne and Queen Mary. Close to the village shop is Lawes Cottage, the 17th-century home of the Lawes family. Henry Lawes (1596–1662) was a well-known musician and composer of the day. He became Master of the King's Musick, wrote the anthem for the Coronation of Charles II and, as a friend of Milton, wrote the music for his *Masque of Comus* in 1634. Next door is Little Clarendon, a handsome, early Tudor manor house with a small 20th-century chapel in the garden. You can view three ground floor rooms, each furnished with vernacular oak furniture. The grandest of all the houses is Philipps House, an imposing stone mansion with a neo-Grecian façade that dominates Dinton Park. Formerly called Dinton House, it was completed in 1820 by Jeffrey Wyatt for William Wyndham, the last of the three great families to reside in Dinton.

## The Penruddockes of Compton Chamberlayne

Overlooking a lovely lake in peaceful parkland, Compton Park (not open to the public) was the seat of the Penruddockes, an influential Wiltshire family for 300 years from 1550. The small 13th-century church contains the family vault and the remains of John Penruddocke, a gallant gentleman who was executed in 1655 following his efforts to raise support against Parliamentarian rule.

## WALK 22 DIRECTIONS

**1** Leave the car park, cross and follow the lane to the B3089. Then turn left, pass the village of Little Clarendon, and continue for 0.25 mile (400m), passing The Wyndham Arms. After this, take the path right opposite a junction and alongside a thatched bus shelter.

**2** Follow the track to a kissing gate and cross the railway line to a further gate. Keep to the track and bear left alongside a stream to reach Dinton Mill. Swing right, to the left of the mill, cross the footbridge over the River Nadder and follow the drive to a lane.

**3** Turn right and follow the metalled lane into Compton

## WHERE TO EAT AND DRINK

Traditional pub food and local ales can be enjoyed at the unpretentious pub, The Wyndham Arms, in Dinton. The Black Dog at Chilmark (west along B3089) is an excellent 16th-century pub with imaginative food and an informal atmosphere.

Chamberlayne. Take the footpath right, opposite the entrance to Compton Park and the church. Ascend steadily. Continue along the track to Home Farm and a junction of tracks.

**4** Turn right, follow the track left around farm buildings and remain on the track with views of the Fovant Badges. Walk beside woodland, then, on nearing the field corner, follow the narrow path into the trees and continue close to the woodland fringe. Pass a covered reservoir to a track.

**5** Turn right and walk downhill to a lane. Turn left then, at the sharp left bend, take the path acutely right and enter a field by a gap (disused stile adjacent). Bear half right to a stile. Cross a tree-lined track, pass through a kissing gate and walk across rough grassland. Within 75yds (69m) move left to another kissing gate.

**6** Turn right along the field edge, go through a kissing gate and bear left down the right-hand side of a field. At a forlorn waymarker, follow the path left, downhill towards Mill Farm, to a stile.

Descend through scrub, cross a footbridge, then a stile and walk ahead to a further stile. Bear left along the river bank, cross a stile and continue to a bridge over the mill stream.

## WHILE YOU'RE THERE

Stroll across Dinton Park and take a closer look at Philipps House (open from late March until October 30th, Mon 1–5pm, Sat 10am–1pm). You can explore the principal ground floor rooms and learn more about the Wyndham family. Note the impressive central staircase of Portland stone and the fine views across the Nadder Valley. Drive west along the B3089 to see Teffont Evias, a charming stone village on the Teff stream.

**7** Pass in front of Mill Farm on a permissive path. Cross a footbridge and stile and bear diagonally right towards the railway. Cross the line via the underpass and bear slightly right to a stile and woodland. Walk through to a stile and keep ahead, to the rear of a barn, to a stile. Continue ahead to a stile, then cut across pasture, between the first and second telegraph poles, to a stile and road.

**8** Cross the stile opposite into Dinton Park and turn right alongside the trees. Bear off left along a grassy path, pass the pond and head towards the church. Go through the first gate on your right and return to the car park.

## WHAT TO LOOK FOR

Note the remarkable series of 12 regimental badges, marked 'Fovant Badges' on the OS map, etched into the chalk on Compton and Fovant Downs as you walk west from Compton Chamberlayne. They were made in 1916 by men who were billeted at huge training and transit camps in the area before going into action on the Western Front. Look for John Penruddocke's name on the family memorial in Compton Chamberlayne church, which states that he was 'beheaded at Exeter'.

# Old and New Wardour Castles

*A gentle ramble through the serene Nadder Valley
and rolling parkland around romantic medieval ruins.*

---

**DISTANCE** 3.75 miles (6km)  **MINIMUM TIME** 1hr 45min

**ASCENT/GRADIENT** 278ft (85m) ▲▲▲  **LEVEL OF DIFFICULTY** ✦✦✦

**PATHS** Field and woodland paths, parkland tracks, 11 stiles

**LANDSCAPE** River valley, undulating parkland

**SUGGESTED MAP** OS Explorer 118 Shaftesbury & Cranborne Chase

**START/FINISH** Grid reference: ST 938264

**DOG FRIENDLINESS** Dogs can be off lead on downland track (Walk 24)

**PARKING** Free parking at Old Wardour Castle

**PUBLIC TOILETS** Old Wardour Castle (if visiting ruin)

---

The austere ruins of Old Wardour Castle stand in a peaceful lakeside setting deep in south Wiltshire countryside. On a spur of high ground, protected by acres of secluded woodland, they overlook the Palladian mansion of New Wardour Castle and the tranquil Nadder Valley.

## Unique Design

Old Wardour was constructed in 1393 for John, 5th Lord Lovel of Titchmarsh and remodelled in 1578 by Sir Matthew Arundell. It was not built as a fortress in the familiar sense of the word but as a tower house as much for comfort and lavish entertainment as for defence. There is no other castle like it in England, hexagonal in shape and with all its rooms and chambers contained within the one building. This unusual design is thought to have been inspired by similar structures in France, where Lord Lovel had been campaigning during the Hundred Years War.

## Civil War Sieges

During the Civil War in 1643, the castle had to be defended against a Commonwealth army. A garrison of only 50 soldiers and servants, along with Lady Arundell, conducted an heroic defence of Old Wardour, holding out for six days against 1,300 of Cromwell's regulars led by Sir Edward Hungerford. The Parliamentarian leader was notorious for depriving the most prominent Royalist families of their houses and property. Lady Arundell surrendered only when offered honourable terms, which the Roundheads immediately broke, sacking the castle and imprisoning her.

Rather than destroy the castle, the Parliamentarians decided to install a garrison there and use it to protect themselves from a strengthening Royalist army in Wiltshire. However, Henry, Lord Arundell's son, resolved to recover his confiscated property and his home. After several unsuccessful demands for the Parliamentarians to surrender, the young Arundell lay siege to the castle in January 1644. During the siege, a gunpowder mine was laid in a drainage tunnel underneath the castle. When it exploded a large portion of the structure collapsed, leaving it uninhabitable.

## Romantic Ruin

Old Wardour was never restored after the war, the Arundell's content to build a smaller house on the south side of the bailey wall. In the early 18th century, the ruins were surrounded by landscaped gardens, creating the flavour of a romantic ruin. Film buffs may recognise the castle as it was used extensively during the filming of *Robin Hood: Prince of Thieves* (1991). New Wardour Castle was designed in a Palladian style by James Paine for the 8th Lord Arundell and built, between 1769 and 1776, on the other side of the park. It remained the seat of the Arundell family until 1944. This fine building has since been a school, and was converted into apartments during the 1990s.

**WALK 23**

## WALK 23 DIRECTIONS

**①** From the parking area, turn left along the drive and pass between the castle and Cresswell's Pond. Pass the Gothic Pavilion, then at Wardour House (private) bear right with the trackway. Gently climb the wide track, skirting woodland, then at a fork keep right. At the end of the woodland, cross a stile by a field entrance and walk ahead along the right-hand side of the field, heading downhill to a stile.

**WHILE YOU'RE THERE**

Visit nearby Tisbury and its magnificent 15th-century stone tithe barn, which at nearly 200ft (61m) long is reputedly the largest in England.

**②** Follow the path beside Pale Park Pond to a squeeze gate, then ascend across the field to a further squeeze gate into woodland. Shortly, bear right to continue along the main forest track, before leaving Wardour Wood beside a gate on to a gravel drive.

**③** At the end of the drive, cross the stile on your right. (For Walk 24 keep ahead along the track.) Head downhill across the field to a metal gate and follow the waymarked path through Park Copse, soon to bear left down a

**WHAT TO LOOK OUT FOR**

In the grounds of Old Wardour Castle (entrance charge), seek out the elaborate rockwork grotto and the remains of a stone circle, both part of the 18th-century landscaping improvements. On Walk 24, a milestone at the top of White Sheet Hill, dated 1736, proves that the track was once the old highway to London.

grassy clearing to a squeeze gate beside a field entrance. Follow the right-hand edge towards Park Gate Farm.

**④** Cross a stile on to the farm drive and turn right (yellow arrow) to cross the concrete farmyard to a gate. Follow the path beside the hedge to a further gate, with the River Nadder on the left, then proceed ahead along the right-hand field-edge to a double stile in the far corner. Bear diagonally left across the field, aiming for the left-hand side of a cottage. Go through a gate and maintain direction to reach a stile.

**⑤** Cross the farm drive and the stile opposite and head straight uphill, keeping left of the tree, towards a stile and woodland. Follow the path right through the trees and soon bear left to pass a building on your left. New Wardour Castle is visible on your right. Keep close to the bushes across the grounds towards the main drive and turn right along a gravel path.

**⑥** Join the drive and walk past New Wardour Castle. Where the track forks, keep right to a stile beside a gate. Follow the grassy track ahead across parkland towards Old Wardour Castle. Climb a stile beside a gate and proceed ahead, following the track uphill to a T-junction of tracks. Turn left and follow your outward route back to the car park.

**WHERE TO EAT AND DRINK**

A short detour leads you to The Forester pub in Lower Street, Donhead St Andrew, for lunchtime snacks or a full restaurant menu: hot drinks are available from the castle ticket office. On Walk 24, White Sheet Hill makes a good picnic spot.

WALK 23

# White Sheet Hill and Ansty

*A longer walk along a breezy downland track to secluded Ansty.*
**See map and information panel for Walk 23**

---

DISTANCE *8 miles (12.9km)*   MINIMUM TIME *4hrs*
ASCENT/GRADIENT *787ft (240m)* ▲▲▲   LEVEL OF DIFFICULTY +++

---

## WALK 24 DIRECTIONS
## (Walk 23 Option)

Having walked to the end of the drive, Point ❸, continue along the track to a lane and turn left through Donhead St Andrew for 1 mile (1.6km) to the A30, Point ❹. Cross over and ascend the zig-zag track up White Sheet Hill. After climbing, continue for 1.5 miles (2.4km) to a road.

The ancient highway up White Sheet Hill follows the crest of chalk downland all the way to Salisbury. Centuries ago it provided dry passage for pilgrims travelling from Salisbury to the abbeys at Wilton and Shaftesbury. In later years it formed part of the coach road from the West Country to London, before the turnpike at the base of the hill.

Cross the road and soon pass a mast installation. Continue for over 0.5 mile (800m), looking for a single pole waymarker on the left, just before hedgerow resumes on the right, Point ❸. Turn acutely left across the field to a gate and turn left to a further gate. Where the fence veers left, turn right steeply downhill to join a path before scrub that descends the scarp face at an angle, left. Go through two gates in the field corner and turn left through a further gate. Turn right along the

field-edge to a stile and continue to a gate and the A30. Turn right, then left along the drive towards Waterloo Farm. Pass between barns, join a track and take the footpath left, between hedges, just before a gate. Just a few paces after a gate on your right, take the path right and descend steeply into Ansty, Point ❻.

Ansty has long been associated with royalty since Alfred and successive kings of Wessex hunted in the surrounding forests. In 1211 the manor title deeds were given to the Knights Hospitallers of the Order of St John of Jerusalem. A Preceptory was formed and they built the Church of St James, the fishpond and a hospice for pilgrims on their way to Shaftesbury Abbey. You can still see the pond, the church and Ansty Manor.

At the lane turn left for the Preceptory or take the lane opposite. Follow it for more than 0.5 mile (800m), then take the path right, opposite a thatched house and beside The Hundred. Walk uphill towards woodland. Skirt right to a stile (concealed by bracken) on the woodland edge. Go ahead and turn left on meeting a track. Turn left at a junction and follow the track to a crossing of paths. Continue ahead along a fenced path between fields. Enter woodland and descend the track ahead to the car park.

# Ebble Valley Wanderings

*Enjoy the unspoilt rural landscape
of the upper Ebble Valley.*

| | |
|---|---|
| **DISTANCE** 5 miles (8km) | **MINIMUM TIME** 2hrs 30min |

**ASCENT/GRADIENT** 377ft (115m) ▲▲▲  **LEVEL OF DIFFICULTY** ✦✦✦

**PATHS** Byways, field paths, bridle paths, metalled lanes, 6 stiles

**LANDSCAPE** Chalk downland and river valley

**SUGGESTED MAP** OS Explorer 118 Shaftesbury & Cranborne Chase

**START/FINISH** Grid reference: ST 964250

**DOG FRIENDLINESS** Let dogs off lead along downland track

**PARKING** On top of Swallowcliffe Down

**PUBLIC TOILETS** None on route

## WALK 25 DIRECTIONS

Of all the valleys that radiate out from Salisbury, the Ebble must be the most peaceful and unspoilt. Time seems to have passed by the valley and its string of tranquil villages, for it's free from busy main roads and their associated developments. This is particularly true in the upper Ebble Valley close to Cranborne Chase and the Dorset border where the 13-mile (21km) chalk stream rises. Here, tortuous narrow lanes link isolated farmsteads, hamlets and villages, hidden and protected in the folds of the steeply rising chalk hills.

Head west along the arrowed byway. Emerge from the copse and take the bridleway left. Descend into the Ebble Valley, keeping to the narrow enclosed path to a gate. Continue ahead down the field-edge, following the track through two gates to Norrington Manor. Cross the track and walk between farm buildings. Norrington Manor and the nearby village of Alvediston

date back to medieval times when they were associated with one of the oldest families in England, the Gawens, said to be descended from the legendary knight Sir Gawain of King Arthur's Round Table. The original manor house was built in the time of Richard II and the Gawens completed the building after 1377. Much of the striking 14th-century stone building still stands, with some 17th-century additions.

Where the track veers right, cross the stile on your left and keep to the left-hand field-edge to a stile in the corner. Cross the track and take the path ahead through the valley bottom to a gate. Keep left-handed through the field to a stile and lane in Alvediston. Turn right, then left along the drive to St Mary's Church. Alternatively, continue along the lane to visit the Crown Inn.

Memorials to the Gawen family, and the Wyndham family who succeeded them at Norrington after 450 years, can be seen in the church which was rebuilt in 1866 and overlooks peaceful water-meadows. Pride of place at the front of the churchyard is the tomb of Sir Anthony Eden (1897–1977), Earl of Avon and Prime Minister between 1955 and 1957. He lived in the brick-built 18th-century manor house close to the church.

Go through the gate on your right and keep to the path ahead across two fields to a gate and enter West End. At the road, turn right across the bridge, then immediately left and follow the lane to a fork. Bear left along Duck Street, then as it begins to dip left, fork right along a footpath to the church in Ebbesbourne Wake.

Ebbesbourne Wake nestles beside the intermittently flowing Ebble stream at the base of the downs, oblivious to 21st-century hustle and bustle. A collection of neat thatched cottages congregates around the 15th-century church, which stands on a hill, and close to the gem of a simple and unspoilt village inn – the Horseshoe.

By the lychgate, bear left to the lane and turn right to visit the Horseshoe. Otherwise, turn left down Duck Street, take the path right, cross the bridge over the Ebble and climb the stile on your left. Follow the path diagonally right up to a stile. Cross the lane and stile opposite, then bear left along the field-edge. Climb steadily, go through the gate on the left and continue ascending

along a track to a gate. Follow the field-edge, crossing two stiles as you pass beside a thicket, then turn right along a byway. At a crossing of tracks, turn sharp left and follow it back to the car parking area.

For hundreds, even thousands of years, this hilltop track, known as the Herepath or Salisbury Way, was one of main highways linking Salisbury to the west, especially for pilgrims travelling to the abbeys at Wilton and Shaftesbury. In later years the route was used by horse-drawn coaches en route from London to Exeter, until improved road-making techniques in the 19th century made it possible for a new road to be built in the Nadder Valley. Its importance in the earliest days can be traced through the presence of earthworks, barrows, tumuli and a little way east, the Iron Age settlement of Chiselbury Camp. It is now a deserted grassy track providing a fine panorama to the north across the broad, undulating and wooded Nadder Valley, and south down steep dry valleys into the narrow Ebble Valley to lofty chalk downland beyond.

# Exploring Bowood Park

*Combine a visit to one of Wiltshire's grandest houses with a walk across its landscaped parkland and along a disued railway.*

---

**DISTANCE** *7 miles (11.3km)* **MINIMUM TIME** *3hrs 30min*

**ASCENT/GRADIENT** *360ft (110m)* ▲▲▲ **LEVEL OF DIFFICULTY** ✦✦✦

**PATHS** *Field, woodland and parkland paths, metalled drives, pavement beside A4, former railway line, 3 stiles*

**LANDSCAPE** *Rolling farmland and open parkland*

**SUGGESTED MAP** *OS Explorer 156 Chippenham & Bradford-on-Avon*

**START/FINISH** *Grid reference: ST 998710*

**DOG FRIENDLINESS** *Keep dogs under contol; off lead along former railway*

**PARKING** *Choice of car parks in Calne*

**PUBLIC TOILETS** *Calne*

---

Like many north Wiltshire towns, Calne rose to fame producing woollen broadcloth and, up until the 18th century, the town had 20 or more mills along the River Marden. Even St Mary's Church owes its splendour to the generous donations of the rich clothiers and wool merchants in the 15th century. When the Industrial Revolution killed its livelihood, Calne turned to bacon-curing and the making of sausages and pies – meat processing had been a major employer in the town from the early 19th century, thanks to its location. Calne was a resting place on the main droving route from the West Country to Smithfield Market. Cattle, sheep and, more importantly pigs, which had been transported from Ireland via Bristol, passed through the town. Harris, the family butchers, took their pick from the grunting mass, eventually establishing their factory here, and in 1864 patented their bacon-curing process. Calne became the home of Wiltshire bacon and further prospered with the arrival of the railway. Now both the railway and Harris have gone, leaving this busy crossroads town with a faded air, although an ambitious plan for reconstructing the town centre is now taking shape. Around the Green are the finest of Calne's Georgian houses, especially Adam House and Bentley House, classic reminders that Calne was once a prosperous market town.

## Bowood House

Leave the town and the busy A4 and head west to the tranquil parkland that surrounds Bowood House, the true focus of your walk. Scenic footpaths take you through the 1,000 acres (405ha) of beautiful parkland, skirting the lake, pleasure gardens and the handsome Georgian house. Originally built in 1624, the house was unfinished when it was bought by the first Earl of Shelburne in 1764. He employed some of the greatest British architects of the day, notably Robert Adam, to design the Diocletion Wing containing the library, galleries, conservatories, a laboratory and a chapel, while 'Capability' Brown laid out the gardens, which are regarded as his best surviving and most satisfactory creations.

# CALNE

In 1955 the original portion of this once magnificent palace had to be demolished, the Lansdownes sacrificing 200 rooms to create a habitable home and preserve the rest of their inheritance. What is left is still impressive, housing a remarkable collection of family heirlooms and works of art. The chief glory of Bowood, however, lies in its pleasure gardens, carpeted with daffodils, narcissi and bluebells in spring. Lawns roll gently down to a long tranquil lake, and there are cascades, caves and grottoes, while terraces, roses, clipped hedges and sculptures are a perfect complement to the house. If you are walking this way between mid-May and mid-June, make sure you explore the spectacular rhododendron walks, more than 2 miles (3.2km) long and not to be missed.

## WALK 26 DIRECTIONS

① Locate the library on The Strand (A4) and walk south along New Road to the roundabout. Turn right along Station Road and take the metalled footpath left opposite the fire station. Turn right on reaching Wenhill Lane and follow it out of the built-up area.

② On nearing a cottage, follow the waymark left and walk along the field-edge. Just beyond the cottage, climb the bank and keep left along the field-edge to a plank bridge and stile. Keep to

77

the left-hand field-edge and soon bear left to a stile. Follow the path right, through rough grass around Pinhills Farm to a stile opposite a bungalow and turn left along the drive.

**3** At a junction, turn sharp right along a further metalled drive and continue for a mile (1.6km). Near a bridge, take the footpath right, through a kissing gate and walk through parkland beside a pond. Cross a bridge, go through a gate and turn right alongside Bowood Lake.

**4** With Bowood House ahead of you, bear left to a gate and cross the causeway between lakes to a gate. Keep straight on up the track, following it left and then right to cross the driveway to Bowood House.

**5** Beyond a gate, keep ahead along the field-edge, soon to

follow the path left straight across Bowood Park. Keep left of trees and the field boundary to a gate. Turn right along the metalled drive beside Bowood Golf Course. Where the drive turns sharp right to a cottage, keep straight on into woodland.

**6** Swing immediately right, then follow the path left, downhill through a clearing (can be boggy) along the line of telegraph poles. Turn left at the bottom of the hill and follow the woodland path uphill beside the golf course. Turn right through a break in the trees and go through the main gates to Bowood House into Derry Hill.

**7** Turn immediately right along Old Road. At the A4, turn right along the pavement. Shortly, cross to the opposite pavement and continue downhill. Pass beneath a footbridge and take the metalled drive immediately right.

**8** Join the former Calne-to-Chippenham railway line at Black Dog Halt. Turn left and follow this back towards Calne. Cross the disused Wilts and Berks Canal and turn right along the tow path. Where the path forks keep right to reach Station Road. Retrace your steps to the town centre.

# Bremhill and Maud Heath's Causeway

*Follow field paths to a hilltop monument
and the start of Maud Heath's impressive Causeway.*

| | |
|---|---|
| **DISTANCE** 4 miles (6.4km) | **MINIMUM TIME** 1hr 30min |
| **ASCENT/GRADIENT** 295ft (90m) ▲▲▲ | **LEVEL OF DIFFICULTY** ✦✦✦ |

**PATHS** Field paths, bridle paths, metalled roads, 10 stiles

**LANDSCAPE** Gently rolling farmland, downland escarpment

**SUGGESTED MAP** OS Explorer 156 Chippenham & Bradford-on-Avon

**START/FINISH** Grid reference: ST 980730

**DOG FRIENDLINESS** Keep dogs on leads at all times

**PARKING** Bremhill church

**PUBLIC TOILETS** None on route

Nestling on the upper slopes of Wick Hill, surrounded by lush pastureland, isolated farmsteads and leafy lanes, tiny Bremhill is a timeless downland village complete with an ancient church, a fine stepped medieval cross and a single street lined with pretty ragstone cottages. Surprisingly, for such a pastoral area, there is much to interest the casual rambler undertaking this short walk, in addition to the absorbing views across the north Wiltshire plain to the Cotswold hills from the mile-long (1.6km) stretch of bridle path across Wick Hill.

### William Lisle Bowles – Rector and Poet

The Reverend William Lisle Bowles (1762–1850), rector of St Martin's Church in Bremhill from 1803 to 1844, lived in the vicarage, now Bremhill Court, adjacent to the church. Bowles was not only an eccentric, filling his garden with grottoes, urns and hermitages and keeping sheep in the churchyard with their bells tuned in thirds and fifths, he was also a poet. His literary friends, such as Wordsworth, Coleridge, Southey and Charles Lamb, were all part of the considerable literary circle centred upon Bowood House. Although much of his poetry was derided, it was his now forgotten sonnets, published in nine editions, that influenced the whole school of poetry and gained admiration from Coleridge and Wordsworth. Scour the churchyard and you will find some examples of Bowles' poetry, as this eccentric vicar was unable to resist breaking into verse on tombstones, monuments and even a sundial!

### Maud Heath

One of Bowles' less impressive verses is inscribed on the monument you will pass on top of Wick Hill. Erected by Bowles and the Marquis of Lansdowne in 1838, it commemorates Maud Heath, a local widow, who in 1474 made a bequest of land and property in Chippenham to provide an income to build and maintain a causeway from Wick Hill through the Avon marshes to Chippenham, a distance of around 4.5 miles (7.2km). Although starting from the top of a hill, much of the land along the route was low lying and prone to flooding in winter, so her aim was to provide a dry pathway for country people to walk to market.

For much of its route the Causeway is little more than a raised path, but the most interesting section can be found at Kellaways, where the way is elevated some 6ft (1.8m) on stone arches as it crosses the River Avon, a remarkable feat of engineering for its time.

On top of the monument on Wick Hill, Maud is depicted in a shawl and bonnet with her basket by her side. Although she has been described as a market woman, it seems unlikely that a lady wealthy enough to provide land and property on this scale would have been walking to market herself. You will see the beginning of the Causeway as you cross the hilltop road, where a tablet states 'From this Wick Hill begins the praise of Maud Heath's gift to these highways'.

## WALK 27 DIRECTIONS

① With your back to the church, turn right and walk downhill through the village of Bremhill. Begin to climb and take the arrowed path left to go through a gate. Proceed straight on below the bank along the field edge to an opening in the corner. Bear diagonally right, heading uphill through two fields to a lane.

## WHILE YOU'RE THERE

Follow the route of Maud Heath's Causeway to Kellaways to view the path where it crosses 60 raised arches and see the sundial monument, erected in 1698 and inscribed with the story of Maud Heath's legacy.

② Cross the stile opposite and cross a paddock to a further stile. Bear slightly left to a stile in the field corner and walk along the left-hand edge to a gate and stile and maintain direction to a stile. In the next field look out for and pass through a gate on your left and head straight across the field to a gate and lane.

③ Turn left, then immediately bear right to a gate. Join the waymarked bridle path along the right-hand field-edge to a gate. Maintain direction through several fields and gates to reach the monument to Maud Heath on top of Wick Hill.

## WHERE TO EAT AND DRINK

The Dumb Post Inn, an 18th-century stone and tile building, provides welcome refreshment towards the end of the walk. Relax in the garden on summer days and enjoy the views towards Bowood Park.

④ Continue to cross a lane via gates, passing the stone tablet and inscription identifying the beginning of Maud Heath's Causeway. Follow the bridle path along the crest of the hill through seven fields via gates and bear left before woodland to reach a gate and lane at the top of Bencroft Hill.

⑤ Turn left, pass Bencroft Farm and a bungalow, then take the waymarked path right, through woodland bearing left on nearing a gate to cross a stile. Proceed straight across the field on a defined path, cross a stile and remain on the path to a stile to the left of a bungalow.

⑥ Turn left along the lane, heading uphill to a junction beside the Dumb Post Inn. Turn right, then left along the drive to a thatched cottage. Go through a squeeze stile and keep to the left-hand edge of the field through a gate and squeeze stile to reach a stile in the field corner. Walk in front of Manor Farm to reach a gate leading into Bremhill churchyard. Bear right along the path back to your car.

## WHAT TO LOOK OUT FOR

On the outside of the north wall of St Martin's Church in Bremhill, you will find a carved stone memorial to 'a poor old soldier', Benjamin Tremblin, who died in 1822 at the age of 92. The verse, written by Bowles, commemorates the notable actions and commanders he had witnessed.

# Heytesbury Chalk Stream

*A gentle stroll alongside the River Wylye and across lush water-meadows.*

DISTANCE 4 miles (6.4km)   MINIMUM TIME 2hrs

ASCENT/GRADIENT 49ft (15m) ▲▲▲   LEVEL OF DIFFICULTY ✦✦✦

PATHS Field paths and bridleways, 9 stiles

LANDSCAPE River valley and lofty chalk downland

SUGGESTED MAP OS Explorer 143 Warminster & Trowbridge

START/FINISH Grid reference: ST 926425

DOG FRIENDLINESS Keep dogs on lead on Walk 28; off lead on downland track on Walk 29

PARKING Plenty of room along wide village street

PUBLIC TOILETS None on route

The River Wylye, one of Wiltshire's lesser-known chalk streams, threads its way through some of the finest downland scenery in the county on its 22-mile (35km) journey from Warminster to Salisbury. Iron Age hill forts, ancient tumuli and barrows litter the rolling chalk downland, much of it now extensively farmed. In the valley, away from the A36, are pretty picture-postcard villages, including the charmingly named Knook, Boyton, Sherrington and Corton, all of which you will visit on Walk 29.

### Historic Heytesbury

Lying just 3 miles (4.8km) east of Warminster, the large village of Heytesbury is an ancient borough with a wealth of history and it is well worth allowing a little time for exploration before or after your walk, if you can resist the homely confines of the Angel Inn!

Wealth and prosperity came to the village through the prominence of one influential family in the 14th century – the Hungerfords – who acquired land and purchased manors across the south-west, including a complex of manors in the upper Wylye Valley. Sir Walter Hungerford fought at Agincourt in 1415 and became Treasurer of England in 1428. He also founded and endowed a chapel in Salisbury Cathedral and founded the Almshouses, or Hospital of St John, that stand opposite the Angel Inn in the village. Under the Hungerfords, the Wylye estates became noted for sheep farming and Heytesbury became the main wool warehouse of the family, who were granted the right to hold a market and two yearly fairs.

Cloth production began in Heytesbury in the mid-15th century but it was not until the 18th century that the proximity of the River Wylye attracted cloth mills along its course. Plans to develop the industry to match that of nearby Warminster never materialised and when its borough status was lost in the Great Reform Act of 1832, Heytesbury gradually declined, the population falling from 1,412 to a mere 454 by 1932.

Sadly, the village lacks buildings of any special interest due to the 'Great Fire' of 1765 which destroyed 65 dwellings along the main street. Notable exceptions include Heytesbury Mill, Parsonage Farm to the south of the church, 69 High Street and Heytesbury House, which stands across the A36 bypass on the site of the medieval mansion of East Court, once the residence of the Hungerford family. In 1926 Heytesbury House became the home of the respected First World War poet and writer Siegfried Sassoon. He grew to love the dramatic views and wide horizons of Wiltshire's downland when he was stationed in the area during training on Salisbury Plain. This inspired him to buy Heytesbury Manor and following his death in 1967, it was occupied by his son George Sassoon until 1994.

## WALK 28 DIRECTIONS

**①** Head east along the village street, pass the Angel Inn and turn right down Mantles Lane. Where it curves right to become Mill Street, take the footpath left along a drive

beside the River Wylye. Bear right on to the footpath in front of Mantles Cottage, go through a kissing gate and walk along the right-hand edge of pasture, soon to bear slightly left on nearing Mill Farm to reach a gate.

**②** Beyond a further gate, turn right across the bridge, then follow the indistinct yellow arrow left and soon cross a footbridge. Fork left at a junction of ways then, just before a further footbridge, turn left through a gap and bear right along the field-edge. At a yellow arrow, bear half left across the field towards thatched cottages to the riverbank and bear right to a stile and junction of paths.

**③** Turn left across the footbridge, pass Knook Manor and St Margaret's Church, then turn right by the post-box and soon pass East Farm on a track (which can be very messy after rain). At two gates, go through the left-hand gate and proceed ahead along the right-hand field-edge to another gate. Continue on into Upton Lovell.

**④** At a crossroads, take the signed footpath right, then just before the drive to Hatch House, follow the path left to a footbridge over the river. Go through a gate and proceed ahead along the field-edge to a metal gate. Turn left through the kissing gate, walk along the hedged path and cross the railway with great care via gates and steps. Continue to a lane in Corton.

**⑤** Turn left through the village, eventually passing the Dove Inn.

## WHILE YOU'RE THERE

Seek out the hamlet of Tytherington across the valley from Heytesbury to view the single-cell chapel that dates from 1083 and was endowed by Empress Matilda, mother of Henry II, in 1140. At Codford St Mary you will find the second largest Anzac War Grave Cemetery in Britain, with the graves of nearly 100 New Zealand and Australian troops who died on the battlefields during the First World War.

## WHERE TO EAT AND DRINK

Both the Angel Inn in Heytesbury and the Dove Inn at Corton offer excellent food and real ale, whilst the Prince Leopold Inn at Upton Lovell also boasts a riverside garden. On the longer route, try the Trough Café at Boyton for home cooked dishes and cakes (Wednesday–Saturday).

At the T-junction, take the arrowed path across the stile on your right. Head across the field on a defined path to a stile and keep ahead through a gate to a further stile. Go along the right-hand edge of the field and shortly, climb a stile, turn left along the field-edge to a stile and pass beneath the railway.

## WHAT TO LOOK FOR

In Knook, note the interesting stone tympanum above the south door of St Margaret's Church. The intricate carved motifs are early 11th century. Boyton church is the resting place of the chivalrous crusader Sir Alexander Gifford, whose striking effigy shows him cross-legged with an otter at his feet. Also in Boyton, look out for the old signs with a religious theme on the exterior of the church and Rectory Cottage.

**⑥** Cross a stile and walk beside the right-hand fence to a gate. From here, follow the grassy track ahead. Cross another stile and keep to the track until you reach a lane. Turn right and follow it through the complex of buildings at Mill Farm and across the river to rejoin your outward route beside the River Wylye back into Heytesbury.

# Wylye Valley Villages

*A longer loop takes you to Sherrington and across breezy downland.*
**See map and information panel for Walk 28**

---

**DISTANCE** *8.5 miles (13.7km)* **MINIMUM TIME** *4hrs*

**ASCENT/GRADIENT** *360ft (110m)* ▲▲▲ **LEVEL OF DIFFICULTY** ✦✦✦

---

## WALK 29 DIRECTIONS
### (Walk 28 Option)

At the crossroads, Point ❹, keep straight on to the church and then follow the path ahead to a drive. Turn left, then left again at the lane, soon to bear off right at the bend on to a bridleway. Enter a field and keep right along the edge to the corner. Keep ahead along a straight path through a tunnel of trees to a field. Proceed straight across towards a bungalow, crossing two stiles to a lane, Point ❹. Turn right and continue across the railway and the River Wylye into Boyton.

Don't miss St Mary's Church in Boyton, approached along an elegant driveway that also leads to the handsome 17th-century manor house. Inside, the Gifford Chapel has a great wheel window. Pevsner described it as 'a tour-de-force'.

At the junction, turn right for the Trough Café, or to visit Boyton church. Otherwise turn left, pass Rectory Cottage then, at a right-hand bend, cross the stile ahead and turn left around the edge of two fields to a gap on your left. Turn right on a drive, then bear left into Sherrington, Point ❹.

Unusually dedicated to two Middle Eastern saints, Cosmas and Damian, the little church possesses some 14th-century glass and an almost complete set of wall-texts used for religious education purposes during the Elizabethan and Jacobean periods.

Turn right through the village, passing the pond, and turn left at the T-junction. In 150yds (137m), cross the stile on the right and walk up the left-hand field-edge to a stile. Turn right and soon bear diagonally left uphill to stile. Continue to a further stile and turn right along the track, Point ❹.

Look back across the valley to view the Rising Sun Badge etched into Lamb Down. At 175ft (53m) by 150ft (46m) tall it is a version of the badge used by Anzac troops and was cut out by Australians stationed at Codford in 1916.

Gradually ascend, keep right on merging with a farm road and continue for 1.75 miles (2.8km) to reach a crossing of routes, Point ❹. Turn right, then almost immediately bear left down a bridle path into Corton. Cross a lane and descend to the lane opposite the Dove Inn. Turn left and join Walk 28 just after Point ❺.

# Devizes and Caen Hill Locks

*A stroll around historic streets
and Rennie's famous flight of locks.*

| | |
|---|---|
| DISTANCE 4.25 miles (6.8km) | MINIMUM TIME 2hrs |
| ASCENT/GRADIENT 180ft (55m) ▲▲▲ | LEVEL OF DIFFICULTY ✦✦✦ |

PATHS Pavements, canal tow path

LANDSCAPE Town streets and canal

SUGGESTED MAP OS Explorers 156 Chippenham & Bradford-on-Avon;
157 Marlborough & Savernake Forest

START/FINISH Grid reference: SU 004617 (on Explorer 157)

DOG FRIENDLINESS Dogs can be off lead along tow path

PARKING Devizes Wharf car park

PUBLIC TOILETS Devizes Wharf

## WALK 30 DIRECTIONS

Devizes is Wiltshire's principal market town and takes its name from the Latin *ad divisas* (at the boundaries), as this old town is at the point where the manors of Rowde, Cannings and Potterne once met. The town grew up around the castle, built by Bishop Osmund of Salisbury in 1080. It burnt down and was rebuilt in 1138 by Bishop Roger of Salisbury, builder of Old Sarum and Malmesbury Castle. The castle was demolished by Cromwell's forces shortly after the Battle of Devizes in 1645 and the present-day building is a Victorian folly.

Devizes has held a market since receiving its first Charter in 1141, so following the demise of the castle, the large market-place became the focal point and the town prospered on the wool trade and dairy produce from the Vale of Pewsey. In the early 19th century, Devizes held the largest corn market in the west of England and also traded in hops,

cattle, horses and cloth. The wool trade's prosperity is mirrored in the wool merchants' 18th-century town houses in St John's and Long Street, and around the fine market place. Interestingly, the pattern of streets originates from when the first castle was built and survives virtually intact. Other notable buildings to seek out are the Elizabethan timber-framed houses in St John's Alley, Great Porch House in Monday Market Street, probably the oldest surviving building in the town, the 16th-century Bear Hotel,

### WHERE TO EAT AND DRINK

Most pubs in Devizes serve Wadworth. Try the friendly Bear Hotel, the Elm Tree in Long Street, and the Castle Hotel in New Park Street. The Bistro (off Market Place) is good for coffee and light lunches. Refreshments are available at the small café above Caen Hill Locks (closed Monday and Tuesday in winter). Just outside Devizes, at Rowde, visit the George and Dragon for innovative pub food, especially fresh fish dishes.

# DEVIZES

**WHAT TO LOOK FOR**

As you stroll through the streets, watch for the regular delivery of the local brew, Wadworth's, by a brewer's dray, pulled by a magnificent pair of Shire horses.

one of a number of historic inns built when Devizes was a major coaching stop, and the two fine Norman churches. Filling the air with the aroma of malt and hops is Wadworth's Brewery, a red-brick Victorian building dominating the northern end of the Market Place. To learn more about the town's history, pick up the Town Trail leaflet from the tourist information centre.

From the car park, walk back down Wharf Street and turn left along New Park Street, passing 18th-century Brownston House and St Mary's Church. At the roundabout, cross the road and walk down Monday Market Street, passing the White Bear. Follow Maryport Street and, on reaching a crossroads, keep ahead along Sheep Street and then Bridewell Street to reach Long Street. Turn right, pass the Wiltshire Heritage Museum, St John's Church and the Town Hall to enter the Market Place. Pop into the Devizes Visitor Centre, then continue along Northgate Street, keeping ahead at the roundabout by Wadworth's Brewery. At the canal bridge, take the path right, signed 'Caen Hill Locks via subway', and join the tow path. Pass under the road and head west to reach the A361. Pass under it and follow the tow path to Caen Hill Locks.

This famous flight is one of the great wonders of the canal era. Completed by John Rennie in 1810, in order to carry the

Kennet and Avon Canal to a height of 237ft (72m), the flight consists of 29 locks in all, extending over 2 miles (3.2km). In the early days, the canal was so busy that gas lighting was installed so that boats could negotiate the locks day and night.

Marvel at this amazing feat of engineering as you descend past the locks and large side pounds. At the bottom, turn round and retrace your steps back uphill, possibly pausing at the tea room across the bridge by the Sir Hugh Stockwell Lock. Recross the A361 and walk back to the subway, leaving the tow path to cross the road bridge and join the northern bank of the canal. Follow the tow path to the next bridge, cross it and turn right to pass the Kennet and Avon Canal Museum at Devizes Wharf.

The canalside at Devizes Wharf has been revitalised in recent years. Signs of industry have gone and the former timbered and balconied granary, built in 1810, is now the headquarters of the Kennet and Avon Canal Trust and houses a small canal museum. The warehouse, now occupied by the Wharf Theatre, was equipped with a huge crane that could unload goods straight into the building from the boats.

**WHILE YOU'RE THERE**

View an interactive exhibition on the medieval origins of Devizes at the visitor centre in the Market Place. Visit the excellent Wiltshire Heritage Museum in Long Street, which boasts one of the finest prehistoric collections in Europe, tracing the history of Wiltshire and its people from the earliest times to the present day.

*Overleaf: The Flight of Locks, Devizes (Walk 30)*

# East Knoyle – Wren's Birthplace

*Savour wonderful views across the Blackmore Vale on this undulating rural ramble around East Knoyle, birthplace of Sir Christopher Wren.*

| | |
|---|---|
| **DISTANCE** 5 miles (8km) | **MINIMUM TIME** 2hrs 30min |
| **ASCENT/GRADIENT** 590ft (180m) ▲▲▲ | **LEVEL OF DIFFICULTY** +++ |

**PATHS** Field paths, woodland bridle paths, metalled lanes, 5 stiles

**LANDSCAPE** Wooded hillside, undulating farmland, village streets

**SUGGESTED MAP** OS Explorer 143 Warminster & Trowbridge

**START/FINISH** Grid reference: ST 879305

**DOG FRIENDLINESS** Can be off lead through woodland and on Windmill Hill

**PARKING** East Knoyle village hall, adjacent to church

**PUBLIC TOILETS** None on route

Sleepy East Knoyle clings to the slopes of a greensand ridge on the northern flanks of the Nadder Valley. Comprising of four distinct hamlets – Underhill, Milton, Upton and The Green – it is an appealing scattered parish characterised by charming stone-built cottages and a myriad of tiny lanes that meet close to Windmill Hill, which at 650ft (198m) offers unrivalled views across the Blackmore Vale into deepest Dorset. This is fine walking country and your rural ramble explores some of the peaceful paths that link the hamlets. It loops round to West Knoyle in the Sem Valley, before ascending Windmill Hill from where, if you time it right, you'll see a magical sunset over the Blackmore Vale.

## The Wren Connection

The heart of the village is Underhill where you will find the post office stores, the ancient Church of St Mary the Virgin, and several reminders that East Knoyle was the birthplace of one of Britain's greatest architects, Sir Christopher Wren. His father, Dr Christopher Wren, was appointed rector of East Knoyle in 1623 and married the daughter of a local squire. The rectory in which they lived now forms part of Knoyle Place, an elegant Georgian house built in 1799. Due to a fire at the rectory, their son Christopher was born on 20 October 1632 in a cottage at the bottom of Wise Lane, opposite the present village shop, Wren's Shop. The cottage was demolished in 1878. Wren's interests lay in mathematics and architecture and his greatest opportunity in the latter came with the rebuilding that followed the London fire of 1666. He re-planned the entire city and supervised the rebuilding of 51 churches, his most famous design being that of St Paul's Cathedral. A stone tablet opposite Wren's Shop records that Wren 'Architect, Mathematician, Patriot' was born in the village.

## Knoyle Church and Rector Wren

The most visible reminder of the Wren family can be seen in the church. Pevsner said that every Wiltshire tourist should make a point of seeing this late 13th-century church, notably the chancel which he describes as

# EAST KNOYLE

'Norman in its bones'. What really makes it interesting are the intricate plaster wall decorations. Designed by Wren's father in 1639, they are unique in an English parish church. Surprisingly, the decorations brought Dr Wren, an ardent Royalist, plenty of trouble during the Civil War. It is said that Roundheads interrupted him working on the plasterwork and thinking he was occupied on idolatrous Papist works of art, they removed him by force and damaged many of the decorations. Although later allowed to continue, he was brought to trial in 1647 accused of 'heretical practices', but doubtless, his real crime was that of being a Royalist. Although the charge of heresy was not sustained, he was fined £40 and his living sequestrated. It is said he returned to East Knoyle and became schoolmaster for five years.

## WALK 31 DIRECTIONS

❶ Turn left out of the car park into the village. Turn left up Wise Lane. Bear left and take the drive right. Keep ahead along the grass track where the drive veers left.

❷ Keep ahead uphill, soon to bear left along a metalled drive. On reaching the stable buildings of Clouds House, take the unmarked path to the right, downhill, passing a garage to reach the lane in Milton. Cross over and bear left along the lower lane.

**3** Pass a thatched cottage on your right then climb the bank, turn right behind a cottage to a gate, and climb through the edge of woodland. At the top, bear half-left along the woodland path and soon descend to reach a bridle path. Turn left, then right at the next junction and follow the woodland path downhill to a lane.

### WHILE YOU'RE THERE

Nine miles (14.5km) west along the A303 is Stourhead, one of the National Trust's finest gardens. Designed by Henry Hoare II and laid out between 1741–80, it is an outstanding example of an English landscaped garden, with classical temples set around a lake and magnificent woodland with exotic trees. Enjoy views of the Palladian mansion on the estate walks (see Walks 43 and 44).

**4** Turn left, then right at the T-junction. Take the bridle path left beyond Chapel Farm, immediately forking right along a track to a gate. Continue along the field-edge, following it left to a gate in the field corner. Gradually descend off Cleeve Hill, passing through two gates and Manor Farm to the lane in West Knoyle.

**5** Keep ahead and continue through the village for 0.5 mile (800m). Pass the village hall and continue to 'Woodside'.

**6** Just beyond turn left through a Woodland Trust gateway towards Mackintosh Davidson Wood. Keep ahead through a metal farm gate, just outside the woodland edge on your right. Continue through two more gates, cross a small valley, and keep ahead through a gap in the hedge to a footbridge with a gate on each side. Bear slightly left past a small woodland spur to a stile in the far hedge.

### WHAT TO LOOK FOR

Note the elegant and appropriately named hilltop mansion, Clouds, as you ascend towards Milton. It was built for the Wyndham family by Philip Webb in 1886 at the cost of £80,000, but had to be rebuilt in 1891 at a further cost of £35,000 after a fire.

**7** Turn right along the track, then left over two stiles and bear diagonally right, soon to descend to a stile and copse. Cross a footbridge and a second stile and keep straight ahead, uphill through the trees to enter a field. Continue beside woodland to a former gateway in the top left-hand corner.

### WHERE TO EAT AND DRINK

The creeper-covered Seymour Arms on the edge of East Knoyle offers generous home-cooked food and Wadworth ales. A short diversion at Windmill Hill will bring you to the Fox and Hounds at The Green for hearty pub meals, a good range of beers and great views from the garden.

**8** Follow the bridleway uphill through woodland. At a junction, turn left, then at the top, bear right into a cul-de-sac to reach the lane. Turn left for the Fox and Hounds. Turn right to reach Windmill Hill, keep ahead at crossroads and descend into East Knoyle. Take the metalled footpath beside Wren Cottage, cross a lane and descend steps into the churchyard. At the road, turn right to get back to the car park.

# Fonthill's Fantastic Folly

*See a grand Gothic folly on this*
*delightful walk across elegant parkland.*

DISTANCE *4.25 miles (6.8km)*  MINIMUM TIME *2hrs*

ASCENT/GRADIENT *278ft (85m)* ▲▲▲  LEVEL OF DIFFICULTY ✦✦✦

PATHS *Tracks, field and woodland paths, parkland, some road walking*

LANDSCAPE *Wooded hillside, rolling parkland*

SUGGESTED MAP *OS Explorer 143 Warminster & Trowbridge*

START/FINISH *Grid reference: ST 933316*

DOG FRIENDLINESS *Keep dogs under control at all times*

PARKING *Lay-by close to southern end of Fonthill Lake*

PUBLIC TOILETS *None on route*

The vast Fonthill Estate lies tucked away on the rolling northern flanks of the unspoilt Nadder Valley between Tisbury, one of Wiltshire's oldest small towns, and the charming village of Hindon. This wonderful short walk explores Fonthill Park, with its beautiful tree-fringed lake and splendid triumphal-style gateway, attributed to Inigo Jones, and ridge-top woodland and pastures between the estate villages of Fonthill Bishop and Fonthill Gifford. Fonthill House lies secluded on a wooded hillside above the sweeping parkland and to the casual passer-by, it is the epitome of a perfect country estate. It is also the setting for the most fantastic story to be found in Wiltshire.

## Fonthill's Eccentric Owner

Fonthill Estate was acquired by William Beckford, a Lord Mayor of London in the mid-18th century. Having built the Palladian mansion, Fonthill Splendens, he died in 1770 leaving a large fortune from sugar plantations to his ten-year-old son William. An utterly spoilt, capricious and extravagant child, England's richest young man embraced Romanticism in all its form, travelling across Europe and writing weird and fantastic tales, notably *Vathek*, a seminal Gothic novel about a hero who lived alone in a mighty tower. Unlike other Romantic writers, the eccentric Beckford had the means to indulge his fantasies.

## Beckford's Great Gothic Folly

Beckford surrounded his estate with a 12 mile (19.3km) long and 12ft (3.6m) high wall, and in 1796 commissioned James Wyatt to build his Gothic dream palace, a grandiose, partly ruined 'abbey', deep in woodland to the west of Fonthill Lake. Beckford and the slapdash Wyatt built in a great hurry, employing 500 men to work day and night, and kept fires burning to prevent plaster and cement from freezing. By 1800, the cruciform building had a central tower 275ft (84m) high and, although unfinished, work had progressed enough for Beckford to entertain Nelson and Lady Hamilton here. Although never completed, the scale of the plan for the abbey was such that the tower was intended to have a spire, elevating it to 450ft (137m), overtopping Salisbury Cathedral by 50ft (15m). Beckford finally moved into the abbey in 1807.

For the next 15 years he lived in the unfinished building as a recluse then, in 1823 when his funds had virtually run dry, he sold the estate to John Farquhar, an equally eccentric gunpowder millionaire, and moved to Bath. Two years later, owing to Wyatt's negligence and dishonest builders, the massive foundationless tower collapsed in a storm, bringing down much of the rest of the abbey. Beckford, meanwhile, was busy building an Italianate tower on the top of Lansdown Hill. Fortunately this didn't collapse and is now the finest surviving example of his work. Fonthill was the classic folly, 'the most prodigious romantic folly in England' as Pevsner described it. Sadly, you are unable to see the abbey remains, a small turret room and the battlemented cloisters, as they are incorporated into a house at the end of a private drive.

## WALK 32 DIRECTIONS

❶ With your back to the lay-by, turn right along the road (this can be busy) that traverses Fonthill Park beside the lake for just over 0.5 mile (800m). Pass beneath the magnificent stone arch and shortly bear right to the B3089. Keep to the right along the pavement into the pretty village of Fonthill Bishop.

**②** Turn right just beyond the bus shelter on to a metalled track. After a few paces, turn left onto a waymarked bridleway through the Old Dairy. Keep left, and join the track that winds uphill towards woodland. Follow the grassy track beside Fonthill Clump and keep to the main track above the valley. In 0.5 mile (800m) fork right downhill into Little Ridge Wood.

**③** At a T-junction, turn left and keep left at the next two junctions, following the wide path to a gate and lane. Turn right through the hamlet of Ridge. Pass the telephone box, walk uphill and bear off right, following the signposted footpath along the drive to Fonthill House.

**④** In 0.25 mile (400m), fork left with the footpath sign to follow a track between paddocks and through a gateway. In 200yds (183m), fork right with a yellow arrow and walk beside woodland. On entering an open field, turn left along the field-edge, turning right at the corner and keeping the hedge on your left to gradually descend towards woodland.

**WHILE YOU'RE THERE**

Enjoy a stroll around Hindon, 2 miles (3.2km) north. Founded by the Bishops of Winchester between 1220 and 1250 and handsomely rebuilt by Wyatt following a fire in 1754, it has a wide attractive High Street lined with stone cottages and two fine inns. Visit Tisbury to see the largest medieval tithe barn in England, situated amidst a fine collection of 14th- and 15th-century buildings at Place Farm.

**WHAT TO LOOK FOR**

Only a wing (a pair of cottages) of Fonthill Splendens remains beside the present Fonthill House. The rest was pulled down by Beckford before he decided to build his Gothic fantasy elsewhere on the estate. Take a closer look at Fonthill Lake. It was used as a location for the filming of Joanne Harris' novel, *Chocolat*, when a mock galleon was deliberately blown up here.

**⑤** Enter the wood and bear left, then right along a gravel track beside Fonthill Lake. Cross the weir to a gate. Disregard the track which goes ahead uphill and bear off right along the lakeside edge. Follow the well-established path through a gate, eventually returning to the parking area.

# Tollard Royal and General Pitt-Rivers

*A walk around Rushmore Park*
*in the heart of Cranborne Chase.*

| | |
|---|---|
| **DISTANCE** 4.5 miles (7.2km) | **MINIMUM TIME** 2hrs 30min |
| **ASCENT/GRADIENT** 616ft (188m) ▲▲▲ | **LEVEL OF DIFFICULTY** +++ |

**PATHS** Field and woodland paths, bridle paths and tracks, 3 stiles

**LANDSCAPE** Chalk downland, sheltered combes, woodland

**SUGGESTED MAP** OS Explorer 118 Shaftesbury & Cranborne Chase

**START/FINISH** Grid reference: ST 944178

**DOG FRIENDLINESS** Can be off lead along Ox Drove and on Win Green Hill

**PARKING** By pond in Tollard Royal

**PUBLIC TOILETS** None on route

Bordering on Dorset, this tranquil corner of south Wiltshire lies in the heart of Cranborne Chase, an undulating tract of chalk downland with breezy ridges and secluded dry valleys or 'bottoms' – one of which hides the village of Tollard Royal. This spectacular walk leads you around the rolling parkland of the Rushmore Estate, formerly the home of the 19th-century archaeologist and ethnologist General Pitt-Rivers, and offers you the option to ascend Win Green Hill, one of the highest points in Wiltshire at 911ft (278m).

## A Royal Forest

Tangled copses and a belt of woodland are all that remain of the great forest that covered an area of some 90 miles (145km). The oldest part, with hunting rights dating back to the time of King John (1167–1216), is centred around Tollard Royal. John hunted on the Chase and owned a small estate at Tollard, hence the 'Royal' in the village name. His lodge was on the site now occupied by King John's House, an elegant Elizabethan manor house near the church. By the 18th century, the forest had become a refuge for poachers, smugglers and vagabonds, and violent, often murderous, disputes arose continually between them and the keepers of the forest. After hunting rights ended in 1828, Lord Rivers destroyed much of the ancient forest, reducing it to more manageable proportions.

## The 'Father of English Archaeology'

General Augustus Pitt-Rivers (1827–1900) inherited the Rushmore Estate in 1880. Winning his rank during the Crimean War, he found fame as a scientist and archaeologist and devoted the last 20 years of his life to excavating archaeological sites on the estate, resulting in five volumes of notes and sketches. He built a private museum in Farnham, 3 miles (4.8km) away, to house his models and local collections. The museum was open every day, free of charge and visited by thousands of people a year. It closed in the 1960s and most of the exhibits went to Oxford University, although you can see scale models, drawings and artefacts in the Salisbury and South

Wiltshire Museum in Salisbury. Pitt-Rivers died at Rushmore in 1900 and you will find a memorial to the family in St Peter ad Vincula Church in Tollard Royal. As you skirt Rushmore Park on your walk, you will glimpse his former home, Rushmore Lodge, through the trees.

## WALK 33 DIRECTIONS

**①** Facing the pond, turn left along the metalled track and take the waymarked path right across the footbridge to a stile. Follow the narrow path half-left uphill through scrub and along the left-hand field-edge. Keep ahead, pass a copse, and bear left through gates into the adjacent field. Keep to the right-hand edge, following a line of electricity poles downhill to a gate and stile.

### WHERE TO EAT AND DRINK

Seek rest and refreshment at the King John pub in Tollard Royal before tackling the energetic longer loop, Walk 34.

**②** Bear diagonally left and steeply descend to a gate and junction of paths in the valley bottom. Take the track right, through a gate and continue to a fork of tracks. Steeply ascend the grassy track ahead and follow it beside woodland for 0.5 mile (800m). Bear right through trees to a metalled lane.

**③** Turn right, then left before the gates to Rushmore Park. Keep to the established track, with cameo views across the park, heading gently downhill to a crossing of paths by the golf course.

**④** Turn right, pass in front of a cottage, and keep to the path alongside the fairway until you reach redundant gate posts. Pass

### WHILE YOU'RE THERE

Visit Larmer Tree Gardens just off the A354 south of Tollard Royal. Created in 1880 by General Pitt-Rivers they contain a collection of Colonial and Oriental buildings, a Roman temple and an open-air theatre. Teas available on Sundays only.

beside the gate posts and keep ahead, soon passing a pond and bearing left beside the woods on your right.

**⑤** Bear right through a gate into the woodland and follow the yellow waymarker sharp right through the trees. At first ill-defined, the path soon bears left to become a clear route (yellow arrows) through Brookes Coppice, to reach a T-junction with a track.

**⑥** Turn left, cross the drive and stile opposite, and bear slightly left downhill to a gate in the field corner. In a few paces, take the second arrowed path sharp right.

### WHAT TO LOOK FOR

In the nave of St Peter ad Vincula Church (St Peter in Chains) in Tollard Royal you will see a 14th-century cross-legged effigy of Sir William Payne who died in 1388. The armour is of banded mail, a rare example found on only four other effigies in England.

**⑦** Follow the track through Tinkley Bottom to a gate and pass below Rushmore Farm. On passing through the second of two gateways, turn immediately left and walk uphill to a pair of gates. Go through the left-hand gate and follow the wire fence on your right through two paddocks to reach a small steel gate.

**⑧** Take the path ahead and bear diagonally right downhill to a gate and the B3081. Keep ahead into Tollard Royal back to the pond and your car.

# To a Wiltshire High Point

*A longer loop takes in Win Green Hill and some memorable views.*
**See map and information panel for Walk 33**

> **DISTANCE** *5.25 miles (8.4km)*   **MINIMUM TIME** *2hrs 30min*
> **ASCENT/GRADIENT** *541ft (165m)* ▲▲▲   **LEVEL OF DIFFICULTY** ✦✦✦

## WALK 34 DIRECTIONS (Walk 33 Option)

Walk along the metalled track, disregard the path taken on Walk 33, then bear right at a fork along the signed 'Byway to Win Green' and steeply ascend the stony track. Remain on this established track as it steadily climbs to the top of Berwick Down. Continue to climb, the track curving left to reach a junction of ways at the summit of Monk's Down, Point **Ⓐ**. Ignore the metalled track on your right and proceed ahead, keeping right at the fork to follow the ancient Ox Drove track along the top of the chalk downland.

Stay on this lofty track around the top of the Ashcombe Valley, and soon reach the cattle grid and National Trust sign at Win Green Hill. Fork left here through a gate and ascend the grassy path to the clump of beech trees at the summit. Keep ahead to the car park at Point **Ⓑ**, and turn left to join the grassy path close to the right-hand fence.

Owned by the National Trust, Win Green Hill is characterised by a steep scarp face and long sweeping slopes, the chalk supporting a rich variety of plant species, including the burnt orchid, round-headed campion and yellow-wort.

Shortly, cross a stile on your right to join the Wessex Ridgeway. Disregard the swing gate on the right and bear left along the field-edge. Follow marker posts steeply downhill through grassland to reach a gate within woodland. Continue straight on and soon turn right along a track. Descend steeply and soon bear left on to the track through Ashcombe Bottom. Keep right and pass Ashcombe Farm.

In 1930 the photographer, designer, painter and writer Sir Cecil Beaton (1904–80) rented Ashcombe House. He is buried in Broad Chalke in the neighbouring Ebble Valley.

Where the track bears right uphill at Point **Ⓒ**, keep straight on. Follow the path in front of a cottage, continuing through a gate and along the valley bottom. As the track curves right to a gate at Point **Ⓓ**, bear off left through a waymarked kissing gate, go through a small metal gate, and turn left along the signposted track towards Tollard Royal. Continue through two further gates back to the pond in the village centre.

# The Battle on Roundway Hill

*Explore the breezy site of a famous CivilWar battle and the ramparts of an Iron Age hill-fort.*

| | |
|---|---|
| DISTANCE | 4.5 miles (7.2km) |
| MINIMUM TIME | 2hrs |
| ASCENT/GRADIENT | 262ft (80m) ▲▲▲ |
| LEVEL OF DIFFICULTY | ✦✦✦ |
| PATHS | Tracks, field paths, stretches of road |
| LANDSCAPE | High chalk downland |
| SUGGESTED MAP | OS Explorer 157 Marlborough & Savernake Forest |
| START/FINISH | Grid reference: SU 013639 |
| DOG FRIENDLINESS | Can be off lead along tracks but under control on farmland |
| PARKING | Car park by The Plantation north of Roundway village |
| PUBLIC TOILETS | None on route |

## WALK 35 DIRECTIONS

Roundway Hill forms a wide ridge of high chalk downland below the summits of Beacon Hill, King's Play Hill and Morgan's Hill, which rise steeply out of the Avon Valley north of Devizes. Now a peaceful scene of wide open fields and grassy scarp slopes affording fine views towards the Cotswolds and Salisbury Plain, this breezy, unspoilt downland once rang with the sound of battle cries. On 13 July 1643, a small Royalist army defeated the Parliamentarians in a bloody skirmish that killed more than 600 troops and saw 1,200 wounded or captured.

It was following an indecisive battle at Lansdown near Bath that the Parliamentarian army, led by Sir William Waller, pursued a weakened Royalist army and their blinded leader Lord Hopton to Devizes where they had occupied the castle and barricaded the streets. Weary, short of ammunition and aware that an unfortified Devizes would not

withstand a siege for long, Hopton sent Prince Maurice to Oxford for reinforcements. Knowing that Hopton's cavalry were in bad shape, yet unaware that Prince Maurice had escaped from the town, Waller took his time in besieging the town as his troops needed rest following the Battle of Lansdown. Eventually, news that Prince Maurice and Lord Wilmot were returning to Devizes with three brigades of cavalry (2,000 men), forced Waller to rally his troops on Roundway Down.

From the parking area take the track across Roundway Hill for 1.25 miles (2km), heading north towards masts on the

# ROUNDWAY HILL

horizon. Along this stretch the track's surface is good and firm underfoot. Swing slightly left to pass the Civil War battle site.

Waller sent out his cavalry, known as 'The Lobsters', to meet Wilmot's brigade and it was here that the two mounted armies clashed. Wilmot's troopers charged twice and forced the Parliamentarians west towards Oliver's Castle. Waller's infantry was unable to fire at the Royalists for fear of hitting their own men.

At a crossing of tracks, turn left along a track, following the Mid-Wilts Way. On passing a barn the track becomes metalled, then in 0.5 mile (800m), at Hill Cottage, fork left. Where the track swings left, keep straight on along a narrow, rutted and often muddy track. Gently ascend and, near the summit, turn sharp left on the Mid-Wilts Way, keeping straight ahead between two fields, with excellent views unfolding to your right. In 400yds (366m), turn right and follow the footpath around the top of the escarpment and around Oliver's Castle, eventually reaching a kissing gate on the left by a steep combe known as Bloody Ditch.

The fleeing Parliamentarian cavalry, unaware of the steep scarp slope on the other side of Oliver's Castle, was chased to the edge and forced down the slope. Many men and horses broke their necks as they plunged over the 300ft (91m) precipice. Others were killed by the newly arrived Royalist infantry who had sallied forth from Devizes on hearing a prearranged gun signal from Lord Wilmot. Since then, this combe has been known as Bloody Ditch and skeletons and military equipment are still occasionally found here.

**WHERE TO EAT AND DRINK**
Take a packed lunch to the picnic site above Bloody Ditch or if you are visiting Devizes, see Walk 30 for refreshment options.

Wilmot's cavalry returned to attack Waller's infantry, who fought on bravely. But, seeing the 2,000 Royalists troops rising over Roundway Down from Devizes, they fled, and many were cut down by the victorious Royalists. The hill was subsequently named Runaway Hill by the Royalists, later becoming Roundway. The defeat of a superior balanced army in proper battle order by a column of cavalry that had ridden down from Oxford was regarded as a remarkable event. As a result of this loss, Waller was unable to replace the Earl of Wessex as Lord General of the Parliamentary army. Also, with no Parliamentary forces left in the West Country, the Royalists had won an important victory.

Walk beside woodland, cross a stile to a parking area and keep straight on along a track, ignoring a similar track right. In 200yds (183m), where the track swings left, turn right and walk along the left-hand field-edge. Gradually ascend, then in the top corner, turn left into a wooded enclosure. Keep ahead, passing to the left of trees. Beyond them you reach the car park where the walk began.

**WHAT TO LOOK FOR**
At the end of the walk, view the newest of the Wiltshire White Horses, the Millennium White Horse cut into Roundway Down in late 1999 to replace the White Horse that had long been overgrown since it was first cut in 1845.

# A Walk with Good Manors from Holt

*Stroll from a rare industrial village
to a beautiful moated manor house.*

| | |
|---|---|
| **DISTANCE** 3 miles (4.8km) | **MINIMUM TIME** 1hr 30min |

**ASCENT/GRADIENT** 147ft (45m) ▲▲▲    **LEVEL OF DIFFICULTY** +++

**PATHS** Field paths, metalled track, country lanes, 6 stiles

**LANDSCAPE** Gently undulating farmland

**SUGGESTED MAP** OS Explorer 156 Chippenham & Bradford-on-Avon

**START/FINISH** Grid reference: ST 861619

**DOG FRIENDLINESS** Keep dogs under control at all times

**PARKING** Holt Village Hall car park

**PUBLIC TOILETS** Only if visiting The Courts or Great Chalfield Manor

Threaded by the busy B3107 linking Melksham to Bradford-on-Avon, Holt is a rare industrial Wiltshire village with a significant history as a cloth-making and leather-tanning centre. The tannery, founded in the early 18th century, still occupies the main three-storey factory in the appropriately named small industrial area – The Midlands – while bedding manufacture and light engineering now occupy former cloth factories. Holt also enjoyed short-lived fame between 1690 and 1750 as a spa, based on the curative properties of a spring, but its popularity declined in face of competition from nearby Bath. The most attractive part of the village is at Ham Green where elegant 17th- and 18th-century houses stand along three sides of a fine green shaded by horse chestnut trees, and a quiet lane leads to the late Victorian parish church with a Perpendicular tower.

## The Courts – Wiltshire's Secret Garden

From the green a walled walk leads to The Courts, a substantial 18th-century house that served, as its name suggests, as the place where the local magistrate sat to adjudicate in the disputes of the cloth weavers from Bradford-on-Avon. Although not open, the house makes an attractive backdrop to 7 acres (2.8ha) of authentic English country garden owned by the National Trust. Hidden away behind high walls and reached through an avenue of pleached limes, you will find a series of garden 'rooms'. Stroll along a network of stone paths through formal gardens featuring yew topiary, lawns with colourful herbaceous borders, a lake and lily pond with aquatic and water-tolerant plants, and explore an area given over to wild flowers among an interesting small arboretum of trees and shrubs.

## Great Chalfield Manor

You will glimpse the Tudor chimneys and gabled windows of this enchanting manor house as you stride across peaceful field paths a mile (1.6km) or so north-west of Holt. Enhanced by a moat and gatehouse, this exquisite group of buildings will certainly live up to your expectations and really must be visited. Built in 1480, during the Wars of the Roses, by Thomas Tropenell,

# HOLT

Great Chalfield is one of the most perfect examples of the late medieval English manor house which, with its adjacent church, mill, great barn and other Elizabethan farm buildings, makes a harmonious visual group.

Sensitively restored in the early 20th century by Sir Harold Brakspear after two centuries of neglect and disrepair, the manor house is centred on its traditional great hall, which rises to the rafters and is lit by windows, including two beautiful oriels, positioned high in the walls. Join one of the guided tours and you will be able to see the fine vaulting, the chimney place of the hall, the concealed spy-holes in the gallery, designed to allow people to see what was going on in the great hall, and the amusing ornaments, gargoyles and other fascinating details of this fine building.

## WALK 36 DIRECTIONS

❶ Turn left out of the car park and then right along the B3107 through the village. Just before the Old Ham Tree pub, turn right along Ground Corner. At the end of the lane take the waymarked path left along a drive. Follow the fenced path beside Highfields to a kissing gate.

❷ Keep to the right along the edge of the field, then keep ahead in the next field towards the clump of fir trees. Continue following the worn path to the right, into a further field. Keep left along the field-edge to a stile in the top corner. Maintain direction to a ladder stile and cross the metalled drive and stile opposite. Bear diagonally left through the field to a hidden stile in the hedge, level with the clump of trees to your right.

❸ Turn right along the lane. At a junction, turn right towards Great Chalfield and go through the kissing gate almost immediately on your left. Take the arrowed path right, diagonally across a large field towards Great Chalfield Manor, visible ahead.

❹ Go through a gate and bear half right down to another gate. Cross a footbridge over the stream, then a stile and bear diagonally left over the field to a gate. Cross the bridge and go ahead beside the hedge to a metalled track by a barn.

❺ Turn right, then right again when you reach the lane, passing in front of Great Chalfield Manor. At the sharp right-hand bend, go through the gate ahead and bear

right, then half-left across the field to cross a footbridge over a stream. Continue walking straight on up the field beside woodland to reach a gate in the field corner.

❻ Follow the left-hand field-edge to a gate, then follow the path straight ahead towards a chimney on the skyline. Go through a gate, bear immediately right to a gate in the hedge and turn right along the path around the field-edge.

❼ Ignore the stile on your right and continue to the field corner and a raised path beside water. Go through a gate and turn left along the field-edge to a further gate on your left. Join the drive past Garland Farm and pass between small factory buildings to the road and turn right back to the car park.

# Castle Combe and By Brook

*Through the wooded By Brook Valley
from a famous picture-book village.*

DISTANCE 5.75 miles (9.2km)   MINIMUM TIME 2hrs 30min

ASCENT/GRADIENT 515ft (157m) ▲▲▲   LEVEL OF DIFFICULTY ✦✦✦

PATHS Field and woodland paths and tracks, metalled lanes, 10 stiles

LANDSCAPE Wooded river valley and village streets

SUGGESTED MAP OS Explorer 156 Chippenham & Bradford-on-Avon

START/FINISH Grid reference: ST 845776

DOG FRIENDLINESS Keep under control across pasture and golf course

PARKING Free car park just off B4039 at Upper Castle Combe

PUBLIC TOILETS Castle Combe

Since being voted 'the prettiest village in England' in 1962, there have been more visitors to Castle Combe, more photographs taken of it and more words written about it than any other village in the county. Nestling deep in a steam-threaded combe, just a mile (1.6km), and a world away, from the M4, it certainly has all the elements to make it a tourist's dream. You'll find 15th-century Cotswold stone cottages with steep gabled roofs surrounding a turreted church and stone-canopied market cross, a medieval manor house, a fast-flowing steam in the main street leading to an ancient packhorse bridge and a perfectly picturesque river.

Yet, as preservation is taken so seriously here, a palpable atmosphere of unreality surrounds this tiny 'toytown', where television aerials don't exist, gardens are immaculately kept, and the inevitable commercialism is carefully concealed. Behind this present-day façade, however, exists a fascinating history that's well worth exploring, and the timeless valleys and tumbling wooded hillsides that surround the village are favourite Wiltshire walking destinations. If you don't like crowds and really want to enjoy Castle Combe, undertake this walk on a winter weekday.

### 'Castlecombe' Cloth

The castle, which gave the village its name, began life as a Roman fort and was used by the Saxons before becoming a Norman castle in 1135 and the home of the de Dunstanville family. In the 13th and 14th centuries the village established itself as an important weaving centre as Sir John Fastolf, the lord of the manor, erected fulling mills along the By Brook and 50 cottages for his workers. With the growth of the cloth trade in Wiltshire, Castle Combe prospered greatly, becoming more like a town with a weekly market and an annual fair.

The greatest tribute to the wealth of the weaving industry is reflected in St Andrew's Church which was enlarged during the 15th century. Its impressive Perpendicular tower was built in 1436. For centuries the villages produced a red-and-white cloth known as Castlecombe. Cloth manufacture began to decline in the early 18th century when the diminutive By Brook

was unable to power the larger machinery being introduced. People moved to the larger towns and Castle Combe became depopulated and returned to an agricultural existence. An annual fair, centred around the Market Cross, continued until 1904, and Castle Combe remained an 'estate' village until 1947 when the whole village was sold at auction.

## WALK 37 DIRECTIONS

**1** Leave the car park via the steps and turn right. At the T-junction, turn right again and follow the lane into Castle Combe. Keep left at the Market Cross, then cross the By Brook and continue along the road to take the path, signed 'Long Dean', across the second bridge on your left.

**2** Pass through a gate and follow the path uphill and then beside the right-hand fence above the valley (Macmillan Way). Beyond an open area, gently ascend through woodland to a stone stile and gate. Cross a further stile and descend into the hamlet of Long Dean.

**3** Pass the mill and, where the lane bears left, follow the track right to cross the river bridge.

*Opposite: The Gallery on the bridge in Castle Combe (Walk 37)*

At a mill house, keep right and follow the sunken bridleway uphill to a gate. Shortly enter sloping pasture and follow the defined path around the top edge, bearing left to reach a stile and lane.

**4** Turn left and descend to the A420 at Ford. Turn right along the pavement and shortly turn right again into Park Lane. (To visit The White Hart in Ford village, take the road ahead on your left, signed 'Colerne'.) Climb the gravel track and take the footpath left through a squeeze stile.

**5** Keep right through pasture and continue through trees to a water-meadow in the valley bottom. Turn left, cross a stile and a stream and steeply ascend the grassy slope ahead of you, bearing left beyond some trees towards a waymarker post. Follow the footpath along the top of the field to a stile and gate, then walk through the woodland to a gate and the road.

**6** Turn left, then immediately left again, signposted 'North Wraxall'. Keep to the road for 0.5 mile (800m) and take the arrowed bridleway, right. Follow the track and then, just before a gate, keep right downhill along a sunken path to reach a footbridge to cross Broadmead Brook.

**7** In 20yds (18m), climb the stile on your right and follow the footpath close to the river. Cross a stile and soon pass beside Nettleton Mill House, bearing right to a hidden gate. Walk beside the stream, cross a stile and you will soon reach the golf course.

**8** Turn right along the metalled track, cross the bridge and turn immediately right again. At a gate, follow the path left below the golf course fairway. Walk beside a wall to reach a stile on your right. Drop down to a metalled drive and keep ahead back into Castle Combe. Turn left at the Market Cross and retrace your steps to the car park at Upper Castle Combe.

# Lacock – The Birthplace of Photography

*Combine a stroll around England's finest medieval village with a riverside walk and a visit to Lacock Abbey.*

---

DISTANCE 2 miles (3.2km)   MINIMUM TIME 1hr

ASCENT/GRADIENT 16ft (5m) ▲▲▲   LEVEL OF DIFFICULTY ✦✦✦

PATHS Field paths and tracks; some road walking, 4 stiles

LANDSCAPE Village and river valley

SUGGESTED MAP OS Explorer 156 Chippenham & Bradford-on-Avon

START/FINISH Grid reference: ST 918681

DOG FRIENDLINESS Dogs can be off lead on riverside pastures if free of cattle

PARKING Pay-and-display car park on edge of Lacock; free to National Trust members

PUBLIC TOILETS Adjacent to Stable Tearooms in Lacock village

---

Timeless Lacock could stand as the pattern of the perfect English village with its twisting streets, packed with attractive buildings from the 15th to 18th centuries, possessing all the character and atmosphere of medieval England. Half-timbering, lichen grey stone, red brick and whitewashed façades crowd together and, above eye-level, uneven upper storeys, gabled ends and stone roofs blend with charming ease.

With the founding of an abbey in the 13th century, the village grew rich on the medieval wool industry and continued to prosper as an important coaching stop between Marlborough and Bristol until the mid-18th century when, as an estate-owned village, time seemed to stand still for nearly 100 years. Entirely owned and preserved by the National Trust since 1944, Lacock is amongst England's most beautiful villages and is, certainly, one of Wiltshire's most visited. If you're interested in architecture and plan to visit Lacock Abbey, allow the whole day and undertake the short stroll.

## Fox Talbot and Lacock Abbey

Of all the outstanding buildings Lacock Abbey, on the outskirts of the village, is the most beautiful. It began as an Augustinian nunnery in 1232, but after the Reformation Sir William Sharington used the remaining structure to build a grand Tudor mansion, preserving the fine cloister court, sacristy and chapter house, and adding a romantic octagonal tower, a large courtyard and twisting chimney stacks in the style of the day.

The abbey passed to the Talbot family through marriage and they gothicised the south elevation and added the famous oriel windows. Surrounded by peaceful water meadows bordering the meandering River Avon, this was the setting for the experiments of William Henry Fox Talbot (1800–77), which in 1835 led to the creation of the world's first photographic negative. You can see some of Fox Talbot's work and equipment, alongside lively and interesting photographic exhibitions, in the beautifully restored 16th-century barn at the gates to the abbey.

# LACOCK

## Village Highlights

Architectural gems to note as you wander around Lacock's ancient streets include the timber-framed At The Sign of the Angel Inn, on Church Street, which retains its medieval layout, a 16th-century doorway and the passage through which horses would pass. Near by, Cruck House, with one of its cruck beams exposed, is a rare example of this 14th-century building method. Further along, you will pass King John's Hunting Lodge, reputed to be even older than the abbey, and St Cyriac's Church, which contains the grandiose Renaissance tomb of Sir William Sharington. In West Street, the George Inn dates back to 1361 and features a huge open fire with a dog wheel that was connected to the spit on the fire and turned by a dog called a Turnspit. Next door to the pub take a quick look at the bus shelter; it was formerly the village smithy.

On the corner of East Street is the magnificent 14th-century tithe barn with fine curved timbers. This was once used to store the rents that were paid to the Abbey in kind, such as corn, hides and fleeces. The building later became the market hall as Lacock flourished into a thriving wool trading centre. Next door is an 18th-century domed lock-up. This is known as a 'blind house', since many of its overnight prisoners were drunks.

You may recognise Lacock's medieval streets as the backdrop to several television costume dramas, notably Jane Austen's *Pride and Prejudice* (1995) and *Emma* (1996), and Daniel Defoe's *Moll Flanders* (1996).

## WALK 38 DIRECTIONS

**1** From the car park entrance, cross the road and follow the gravel path into the village, passing the entrance to Lacock Abbey and the Fox Talbot Museum. Turn right into East Street opposite the Red Lion and walk down to Church Street. Turn left, pass At The Sign of the Angel with its magnificent 16th-century doorway and bear left into West Street to opposite the George Inn. Shortly, follow the road left into the High Street.

**2** Pass the National Trust shop and turn left to walk back down East Street. Turn right along Church Street and turn left at Nethercote, in front of St Cyriac's Church, to reach an ancient packhorse bridge beside a ford across the Bide Brook. Follow the path beside the stream, then up a lane beside cottages to reach the end of the road.

**3** Go through the kissing gate on your right and follow the tarmac path across the field to a gate. Pass the stone cottages at Reybridge to a lane. Turn right along the lane, then right again to cross the bridge over the River Avon.

**4** Immediately cross the stile on your right and bear diagonally left to the far corner where you rejoin the riverbank to reach a kissing gate. Walk beside the river

for 200yds (183m) to a stile, and cross the field following the line of electricity poles to a gate. Keep straight on to a stile beside a gate, and then head towards the stone bridge over the Avon.

**5** Climb the stile and turn right across the bridge. Join the raised pavement and follow it back into the village and car park.

# Bowden Park

*A longer loop takes in a disused
canal and Bowden Park.*
**See map and information panel for walk 38**

---

**DISTANCE** *5.5 miles (8.8km)* **MINIMUM TIME** *2hrs 30min*

**ASCENT/GRADIENT** *426ft (130m)* ▲▲▲ **LEVEL OF DIFFICULTY** +++

---

## WALK 39 DIRECTIONS
## (Walk 38 Option)

Cross the river bridge at the end
of the directions for Point ❸ of
Walk 38, and take the stile on
your left. Bear diagonally right
across the field to a stile and cross
the lane and stile opposite. Follow
the path to two stiles and turn
left around the field-edge. Climb
the stile on your left and turn
right along the field edge. After
200yds (183m) continue along
the remains of the Wilts and Berks
Canal, which soon joins National
Cycle Route 4 along the tow path.

The canal was opened in 1810 and
linked Semington, on the Kennet
and Avon Canal to Abingdon and
the Thames in Oxfordshire, a
distance of 51 miles (82km) with
42 locks. Coal from Somerset was
the main cargo until the canal was
formally abandoned in 1914.

Pass a restored bridge at Point
Ⓐ; then, just before a gate across
the cycleway, turn right over two
stiles and follow the winding path
through woodland to a stile. Keep
ahead across the field to a gate,
and maintain direction across the
next field to a gate. Join a track
along the left-hand field-edge,
cross a farm drive and continue
to a gate. Ascend the track to a
gate and proceed uphill towards
a house.

Before a gate turn right, Point Ⓑ,
(field entrance left) across the top
of the field below a house to reach
double stiles. Bear half-right, then
left, to a gate beside a cattle grid
and ascend the farm drive through
woodland, then continue uphill to
a gate. Ignore the farm drive right
and continue to the lane. Turn left,
then cross the stile on the right
before a house, Point Ⓒ. Keep
to the left-hand edge of the field,
cross a stile and bear diagonally
left across the field to a stile in the
corner. Cross the stile ahead into
woodland and follow the path to a
stile. Proceed ahead along the field
edge to reach a stile on your right.
Bear half-left across Bowden Park,
and bear right down a track to a
stile by a gate, Point Ⓓ.

Keep ahead downhill to a stile and
turn left around the field-edge
to another stile and a gate near
a house. Follow the path to the
drive and follow it left. As tarmac
gives way to gravel, bear off right
across Bewley Common to the
road junction. Turn right and keep
to the road to cross the River
Avon and return to Lacock.

# Malmesbury and the Avon

*An undemanding riverside stroll around a Saxon hilltop town.*

| | |
|---|---|
| DISTANCE | 2 miles (3.2km) MINIMUM TIME 1hr |
| ASCENT/GRADIENT | 49ft (15m) ▲▲▲ LEVEL OF DIFFICULTY +++ |
| PATHS | Field paths, town streets, 3 stiles |
| LANDSCAPE | River valley and urban area |
| SUGGESTED MAP | OS Explorer 168 Stroud, Tetbury & Malmesbury |
| START/FINISH | Grid reference: ST 932875 |
| DOG FRIENDLINESS | No problems on riverside pastures |
| PARKING | Yard car park (fee-paying) |
| PUBLIC TOILETS | Malmesbury town centre |

## WALK 40 DIRECTIONS

A picturesque town of mellow Cotswold stone, Malmesbury stands between two branches of the River Avon on the site of a Saxon fortified hilltop town. Dominating the surviving medieval street plan are the remains of a Benedictine abbey, founded in the 7th century AD by St Aldhelm, its first abbot. Malmesbury is one of the oldest boroughs in England, the original royal charter was granted by King Alfred in AD 880 and confirmed by King Athelstan (reigned AD 925–939), when he made Malmesbury his capital, holding court just outside of the town.

After the dissolution of the monasteries in the 1540s, the abbey was sold for £1,517 to local wool merchant, William Stumpe, who presented the surviving nave to the townspeople for their parish church. In the following centuries several mills sprang up along the local rivers and the town became an important centre for the manufacture of woollen cloth.

It later became renowned for producing fine lace and silk.

From the car park, keep the river to your right and walk towards the abbey and Abbey House. At the information board, bear left, then right through a kissing gate into Conygre Mead. Keep right along the path and walk along the river bank, noting the old railway tunnel and Abbey House across the river.

### WHERE TO EAT AND DRINK

Try the Summer Café for tasty snacks and lunches. Excellent coffee, afternoon teas and light lunches are also served in the Old Bell Hotel.

Abbey House, a handsome Tudor building, was built by William Stumpe in the mid-16th century on monastic foundations. It has a 5-acre (2ha) garden featuring one of Britain's largest private collections of roses.

At the road, turn right across the bridge and descend steps to reach a stile. Keep right across

Longmead to the remains of a railway line in the right-hand field corner. Take the left-hand path through the next field and walk along the river bank to a stile and footbridge. Cross the old sluice gate and continue to the lane beside Wynyard Mill. Turn right past the bowls club, following St John's Street to Lower High Street.

St John's Street has many ancient houses, notably a collection of almshouses from 1694 built on the site of St John the Baptist's Hospital. Incorporated in the gable wall is an early 13th-century arch. The Old Courthouse, through School Arch, is where the Old Corporation of Burgesses and Commoners have met since 1616. These are direct descendants of the men living in Malmesbury more than 1,000 years ago to whom King Athelstan gave 500 acres (202.5ha) of common land (King's Heath) for their help in the battle against the Danes, and this land is still passed down the generations.

Cross the road and go through the memorial gates and bear left along the walkway parallel to St John's Bridge to rejoin the road opposite Avon Mills. Turn right along the pavement and go through the gate on your right to follow the permissive path beside the River Avon. Cross a stile and keep to the path through gates and across various footbridges, soon to leave the river, keeping beside the hedge to a gap in the field corner and a small stone bridge.

Cross the bridge, where the path becomes paved, to reach a footbridge across the Avon. At a T-junction, turn left along Burnivale, then climb Betty Geezers Steps on your right to reach Abbey Row, with the Civic Trust Garden to your left. Cross the road and bear right in front of the Old Bell Hotel and enter the close to visit the abbey.

On the far side of Abbey Close is the 500-year-old Market Cross, an elaborate, octagonal building with a ribbed ceiling and intricate carvings, which was built for the market traders and buyers to stand in when it rained. The isolated steeple is the remnant of the 13th-century St Paul's Church, the parish church until 1541. This now serves as the bell tower for the abbey church. Among the more striking features of the abbey are the Norman porch, one of the finest in England, ablaze with exquisite carvings, the vaulted nave roof, the 14th-century stone screens in the north and south aisles, and the tomb of King Athelstan.

Return to the Old Bell and take the path immediately right for the Cloister Garden. Walk through the garden and turn left down steps, then right along Mill Lane back to the car park.

# Sherston and Easton Grey's Cotswold Fringe

*The infant Bristol Avon links attractive stone villages on this pastoral ramble on the south-eastern fringes of the Cotswolds.*

WALK 41

---

DISTANCE 6.5 miles (10.4km)   MINIMUM TIME 3hrs

ASCENT/GRADIENT 131ft (40m) ▲▲▲   LEVEL OF DIFFICULTY ✦✦✦

PATHS Field and parkland paths, tracks, metalled lanes, 13 stiles

LANDSCAPE River valley and gently rolling farmland

SUGGESTED MAP OS Explorer 168 Stroud, Tetbury & Malmesbury

START/FINISH Grid reference: ST 853858

DOG FRIENDLINESS Dogs can be off lead along Fosse Way

PARKING Sherston High Street; plenty of roadside parking

PUBLIC TOILETS None on route

---

The Bristol Avon rises in the foothills of the Cotswolds in the north-west corner of Wiltshire and is little more than a wide and shallow stream as it flows through the gently rolling pastoral countryside west of Malmesbury. Despite its size, this peaceful river enhances all the charming little stone villages in this unspoilt and somewhat forgotten area of north Wiltshire, which is typically Cotswold in appearance and character. In fact, 18 villages between Colerne and Malmesbury are officially part of the Cotswold Area of Outstanding Natural Beauty. Of these, Sherston must rank among the most attractive, with its wide High Street, doubtless once used as a market, lined with some interesting 17th- and 18th-century buildings. Sherston was a borough by the 15th century and prospered as a result of the flourishing wool trade at the time. It still has the feel of a market town, with narrow back streets and alleys, and continues to be a thriving community despite becoming a dormitory village.

## Legend of a Local Hero

It has been suggested that Sherston is Sceorstan, as chronicled by Henry of Huntingdon, where in 1016 Edmund Ironside won a battle against the Danes who were led by King Canute. The early legend of John Rattlebone, a local yeoman promised land by Ironside in return for service against the Danes, is deep rooted. Sadly, this brave knight was terribly wounded in battle and although he staunched his bleeding with a stone tile and continued fighting, he reputedly died as Canute's army withdrew. Other traditions say Rattlebone survived to claim his reward.

In the 17th century, the antiquary John Aubrey recorded the following local rhyme: 'Fight well, Rattlebone, Thou shalt have Sherston, What shall I with Sherston do, Without I have all belongs thereto? Thou shalt have Wych and Wellesley, Easton Town and Pinkeney.' Later traditions tell us that the small stone effigy on the south side of the porch outside the parish church is that of Rattlebone, and that an ancient timber chest in the church, marked with the initials R B, is where Rattlebone kept his armour. Whatever the truth is, the Rattlebone Inn opposite the church keeps his name alive.

# SHERSTON

## Easton Grey – Pure Cotswold Charm

Peaceful parkland and riverside paths lead you downstream to picturesque Easton Grey. Set around a 16th-century stone bridge and climbing a short, curving street is an intimate huddle of ancient stone houses, with mullioned windows, steep, lichen-covered roofs and colourful, flower-filled gardens that touch the river bank. Set back on a rise above the river is Easton Grey House, a handsome 18th-century manor house with a classical façade and portico, surrounded by elegant gardens and lovely valley views. It was the summer retreat of Herbert Asquith, 1st Earl of Oxford, when he was Prime Minister between 1908 and 1916.

## WALK 41 DIRECTIONS

❶ On Sherton's High Street, walk towards the village stores, pass the Rattlebone Inn and turn right into Noble Street. Pass

Grove Road and take the footpath left up a flight of steps. Cross a cul-de-sac and follow the metalled footpath to a gate. Continue at the rear of houses to a further gate.

**2** Bear diagonally right across a field to a stile, followed by a gate leading out to a lane. Turn right, cross the river and turn left, signed 'Foxley'. At the end of woodland on your left, take the footpath left through a gate. Follow the track across Pinkney Park to a gate.

**3** Keep ahead, bearing left beside the wall to a gate. Immediately beyond it turn right for several paces, then left through a gate. Follow the path round the edge of a field to a stile. Cross it, then go immediately right over the adjacent stile. Aim for the left-hand corner of the field to the next stile. Keep alongside the fence to the next stile and bear right to a gate.

### WHERE TO EAT AND DRINK

Rest and refuel at the lively Rattlebone Inn in Sherston. The rambling bars are the setting for hearty lunchtime snacks and imaginative evening meals with decent wine and Youngs ales. Alternatively, try the Carpenters Arms which is noted for fish.

**4** Go diagonally across the field with Easton Grey House visible in the distance. Cross two stiles with a footbridge in between and head downhill to a gate and lane.

**5** Turn left into Easton Grey. Cross the river bridge, turn right uphill to take the footpath ahead on reaching entrance gates on your right. Cross a gravelled area, go through a gate and keep ahead to a stile. Maintain direction across the next field and gently descend to follow a track into the next field.

**6** Turn right along the field-edge and bear off right in the corner, downhill through scrub to

### WHAT TO LOOK OUT FOR

The wide, hedged and dead-straight track that you follow on your return to Sherston is the Fosse Way. This ancient Roman road ran from Lincoln to Exeter and is so named because it was bordered on both sides by a 'fosse' or ditch.

a footbridge. Keep ahead beside a ruin to a gate. Cross a stile and continue to a further stile and gate. Follow the track downhill to a stile and turn right along a track (Fosse Way). Continue for just over 0.5 mile (around 900m) to a road.

**7** Cross straight over and keep to the byway to another road. Bear left and keep ahead where the lane veers sharp left. Follow this rutted track for 0.5 mile (800m), then cross the arrowed stile on your right. Head across the field to a stile and continue ahead beside a hedge to a gate. Turn right then immediately left, skirt a paddock and join a track.

**8** Cross a racehorse gallop to a gate. Walk through scrub to another gate and keep to the track ahead to a road. Turn left and continue to a crossroads. Proceed straight on to the next junction and keep ahead, following the lane all the way back into Sherston.

### WHILE YOU'RE THERE

Nearby Luckington Court Gardens, a BBC TV location for Jane Austen's *Pride and Prejudice* (1995), has a 3-acre (1.2ha) formal garden and a walled flower garden. Head north just across the border into Gloucestershire to visit Westonbirt Arboretum, one of the finest and most important collections of trees and shrubs in the country.

# Brunel's Great Tunnel Through Box Hill

*A hilly walk around Box Hill, famous for its stone
and Brunel's greatest engineering achievement.*

DISTANCE 3.25 miles (5.3km)   MINIMUM TIME 1hr 45min

ASCENT/GRADIENT 508ft (155m) ▲▲▲   LEVEL OF DIFFICULTY ✦✦✦

PATHS Field and woodland paths, bridleways, lanes, 16 stiles

LANDSCAPE River valley and wooded hillsides

SUGGESTED MAP OS Explorer 156 Chippenham & Bradford-on-Avon

START/FINISH Grid reference: ST 824686

DOG FRIENDLINESS Can be off lead on Box Hill Common and in woodland

PARKING Village car park near Selwyn Hall

PUBLIC TOILETS Opposite Queens Head in Box

Box is a large straggling village that sits astride the busy A4 in hilly country halfway between Bath and Chippenham. Although stone has been quarried here since the 9th century AD, Box really found fame during the 18th century when the local stone was used for Bath's magnificent buildings. The construction of Box Tunnel uncovered immense deposits of good stone and by 1900 Box stone quarries were among the most productive in the world. Little trace can be seen above ground today, except for some fine stone-built houses in the village and a few reminders on Box Hill.

### Appointed Engineer

In 1833, the newly created Great Western Railway appointed Isambard Kingdom Brunel (1806–59) as engineer. His task was to build a railway covering the 118 miles (190km) from London to Bristol. The problems and projects he encountered on the way would help to make him the most famous engineer of the Victorian age. After a relatively straightforward and level start through the Home Counties, he came to the hilly Cotswolds.

### Brunel's Famous Tunnel

The solution at Box would be a tunnel, and at nearly 2 miles (3.2km) long and with a gradient of 1:100 it would be the longest and steepest in the world at the time. It would also be very wide. Already controversial, Brunel ignored the gauge of other companies, preferring the 7ft (2.1m) used by tramways and roads (and, it was believed, Roman chariots). He also made the tunnel dead straight, and, never one to 'hide his light', the alignment was calculated so the dawn sun would shine through on his birthday on 9th April. Unfortunately he did not allow for atmospheric refraction and was two days out!

### Passage to Narnia?

All was on a grand scale: a ton of gunpowder and candles were used every week, 3 million bricks were fired to line the soft Cotswold limestone and 100 navvies lost their lives working on the tunnel. After two and a half years the way was open, and although Brunel would ultimately lose the battle of the gauges, his magnificent line meant that Bristol was then a mere two hours from the capital. Although artificial, like many large dark holes, the tunnel has collected its fair share of mystery with tales of noises, people under the hill and trains entering the tunnel, never to re-emerge. But as is often the case, the explanations are rather more mundane. To test excavation conditions, Brunel dug a small trial section alongside what is now the eastern entrance and the military commandeered this section during the Second World War as a safe and fairly secret store for ammunition, records and top brass. Sadly it is not a passage to Narnia!

## WALK 42 DIRECTIONS

**1** Facing the recreation ground, walk to the left-hand side of the football pitch to join a track in the corner close to the railway line. When you reach the lane, turn left, pass beneath the railway, cross a bridge and take the arrowed footpath, to the right, before the second bridge.

**2** Walk beside the river, cross a footbridge and turn right. Cross a further footbridge and continue to a stile. Walk through water-meadows close to the river, then go through a gate and maintain direction. Shortly, bear left to reach a squeeze stile in the field corner. Follow the right-hand field-edge to reach a stile leading on to a lane.

# BOX

**3** Turn right, then right again at the junction. Cross the river, pass Drewett's Mill and steeply ascend the lane. Just past Mills Platt Farm, take the arrowed footpath ahead across a stile. Continue steeply uphill to a stile and cross the A4. Ascend steps to a lane and proceed straight on up Barnetts Hill. Keep right at the fork, then right again and pass the Quarryman's Arms.

**4** Keep left at the fork and continue beside Box Hill Common to a junction. Take the bridleway straight ahead into woodland. Almost immediately, fork left and follow the path close to the woodland edge. As it curves right into the beech wood, bear left and follow the path through the gap in the wall and then immediately right at the junction of paths.

**5** Follow the bridle path to a fork. Keep left, then turn right at the T-junction and take the path left to a stile. Cross a further stile and descend into Thorn Wood, following the stepped path to a stile at the bottom.

**6** Continue through scrub to a stile and turn right beside the fence to a wall stile. Bear right to a further stile, then bear left uphill to a stile and the A365. Cross over and follow the drive ahead. Where it curves left by stables, keep

ahead along the arrowed path to a house. Climb a few steps, bear right to pass Washwell cottage and follow the drive uphill to a T-junction.

**7** Turn left, then on entering Henley, take the path right, across a stile. Follow the field-edge to a stile and descend through a paddock to a stile. Continue to a stile and gate.

**WHAT TO LOOK OUT FOR**

Explore Box and locate the Blind House on the main street, one of a dozen in Wiltshire for disturbers of the peace. Look for Coleridge House, named after the poet who often broke his journey here on his way to Nether Stowey. Also look for the former Candle Factory on the Rudloe road that produced the candles used during the building of Box Tunnel, and head east along the A4 for the best view of the tunnel's entrance.

**8** Follow the drive ahead, bear left at the garage and take the metalled path right, into Box. Cross the main road and continue to the A4. Turn right, then left down the access road back to Selwyn Hall.

**WHERE TO EAT AND DRINK**

In Box, you will find both the Queen's Head and The Bear offer good food and ale in convivial surroundings. Time your walk for opening time at the Quarryman's Arms on Box Hill. Enjoy the views across Box from the dining room with a pint of locally brewed ale.

# Stourhead's Paradise

*A gentle walk through the idyllic setting of Stourhead Estate.*

WALK 43

---

DISTANCE 3 *miles (4.8km)* MINIMUM TIME *1hr 30min*

ASCENT/GRADIENT 262ft (80m) ▲▲▲ LEVEL OF DIFFICULTY ✦✦✦

PATHS *Parkland and woodland paths and tracks, 3 stiles*

LANDSCAPE *Woodland and parkland*

SUGGESTED MAP *OS Explorers 142 Shepton Mallet; 143 Warminster & Trowbridge*

START/FINISH *Grid reference: ST 779340 (on Explorer 142)*

DOG FRIENDLINESS *Under control at all times. No dogs in Stourhead Gardens February–October*

PARKING *Free National Trust car park at Stourton*

PUBLIC TOILETS *Stourhead Visitor Centre and Spread Eagle courtyard*

---

Although without the immediate charm of villages like Lacock and Castle Combe, Stourton enjoys an idyllic setting in a valley on the edge of the Stourhead Estate. Beautifully preserved, consisting of a pleasing group of 18th-century cottages, an inn, St Peter's Church and a graceful medieval cross, its unique atmosphere is attributable to the glorious views across a lake and one of Europe's finest landscaped parkland gardens.

Wealthy banker Henry Hoare acquired Stourhead in 1717. He promptly pulled down medieval Stourton House, and commissioned Colen Campbell, the foremost architect and designer of the day, to build a new Palladian style house. Extended in the 1780s by Sir Richard Colt Hoare, the magnificent interior includes an outstanding Regency library, a significant collection of Chippendale furniture and fine paintings in the elegant gallery.

### A Taste of Paradise

But Stourhead is more famous for its gardens, designed by Henry Hoare II and laid out in four years from 1741. Now National Trust, they are an outstanding example of the English landscape style. Inspired by Italian landscapes and by the artists Claude Lorraine and Nicholas Poussin, Hoare set out to create a poetic landscape at Stourhead. Having dammed the River Stour and diverted the medieval fish ponds to create a large lake, he began his three-dimensional 'painting', planting beechwoods to clothe the hills and frame new lakes. Classical temples, including the Pantheon and the Temple of Apollo, were located around the central lake at the end of a series of vistas, which change as you stroll around the estate. The gardens are a memorable place to visit at any time, but in spring the rhododendrons and azaleas are spectacular and the autumnal colours are beautiful.

This walk explores the surrounding farmland and woodland. Along the way, at Park Hill, you will cross a large bank, formerly the boundary to the original deer park created in 1448 by John Stourton, and pass an Iron Age hill-fort covering 6 acres (2.4ha).

WALK 43

232

Neolithic
Enclosure **B**

245

Iron Age
Hill Fort

White
Sheet
Hill

**P**

← Frome

B3092

**P**

Red Lion
Inn

Beech
Clump

190

**C**

Search
Farm

LONG LANE

**A**

Drove
Lodge

**Stourton**

**7**

B3092

Mere →

King Alfred's
Tower

Stourhead
House

**6**

200

Stourhead
Gardens

**P 1**

Visitor Centre

The
Obelisk

Spread Eagle Inn

✝ St Peter's Church

*Garden
Lake*

185

Six Wells
Bottom

**2**

Rock Arch

**5**

Hill Fort

**4**

215

Beech
Cottage

**3**

Park
Hill

170

Ruins of
Tucking Mill

0 ½ mile

0 500m

## WALK 43 DIRECTIONS

**1** Leave the car park via the exit and turn left down the lane into Stourton village passing the Spread Eagle Inn, St Peter's Church and the entrance to Stourhead Gardens. (Note: National Trust members or those paying to visit the Gardens and Stourhead House should access the village via the visitor centre.) Continue along the lane, pass beneath the Rock Arch and turn immediately right along a track.

### WHERE TO EAT AND DRINK
Adjacent to the car park is the National Trust's restaurant serving teas, coffees and light lunches. Alternatively, enjoy a pint and a ploughman's at the Spread Eagle Inn in the village or stop at the Red Lion below White Sheet Hill.

**2** Pass beside the lake, cross a cattle grid and follow the track to Beech Cottage. Keep left along the track, to a stile beside a gate and ignore the Stour Valley Way signposted to the right. At a fork, bear right through the gate, signed 'Alfred's Tower'.

**3** Proceed ahead on the grassy track along the top of the field to a further gate and stile, noting the ruins of Tucking Mill and cottages on your left. Walk through the woodland and take the first track right (by a silver National Trust sign) into coniferous woodland. Ascend steeply to reach Broad Ride, a wide grassy swathe through the woodland.

**4** Turn left to a gate and the Iron Age hill-fort at Park Hill. Do not cross the stile, but bear right along the narrow path beside the fence to reach a track. Turn right and shortly turn sharp left downhill

through the woodland to reach a stile and Six Wells Bottom.

**5** Turn right and bear diagonally left across the valley bottom, keeping left of the lake, heading uphill to a gate on the edge of woodland. Continue up the track to a gate and turn immediately left up the bank to pass the Obelisk, with Stourhead House clearly visible now to your right.

**6** On reaching the track, turn right towards Stourhead House. At a junction of tracks, turn right through a gate and pass in front of the house. Walk down the drive then, where it curves right, take the waymarked path left through a gate to start of Walk 44.

### WHILE YOU'RE THERE
Don't miss climbing King Alfred's Tower on the edge of the Stourhead Estate (open March to October). This intriguing red-brick folly, built in 1772, stands 160ft (49m) high and affords magnificent views across Somerset, Dorset and Wiltshire.

**7** To finish this short loop (Walk 43), pass underneath the gate house and turn left up the lane back to the car park. National Trust members and visitors that have paid to enter the Stourhead gardens and house can bear right just before the gatehouse and walk through the walled garden and across a bridge to return to the car park via the visitor centre.

### WHAT TO LOOK FOR
In Beech Clump below White Sheet Hill, look out for the memorial dedicated to the airmen who lost lost their lives in Dakota TS436 No 107OTU Leicester East, which crashed here after taking off from RAF Zeals on 19th February 1945.

*Opposite: View from the top of King Alfred's Tower (Walk 43)*

# White Sheet Hill

*A longer loop to a neolithic camp
and a hill-fort on White Sheet Hill.*
**See map and information panel for Walk 43**

---

**DISTANCE** *5 miles (8km)*   **MINIMUM TIME** *2hrs 30min*

**ASCENT/GRADIENT** *344ft (105m)* ▲▲▲   **LEVEL OF DIFFICULTY** +++

---

## WALK 44 DIRECTIONS
(Walk 43 Option)

From the gate, Point **7**, beside the main drive follow the path straight across the parkland in front of Stourhead House. Merge with a track and keep ahead through two gates to a lane. Cross the stile opposite and bear half-left across a field to a stile located between electricity poles. Climb a further stile and continue ahead to the left of a hedge, following the grass track to a stile in the corner, Point **A**. Drop down steps and turn right along the sunken bridleway (Long Lane) to reach the B3092, opposite the Red Lion Inn. Cross straight over and follow the lane towards White Sheet Hill. Pass a parking area and continue steeply uphill, following the track sharp right to pass through the neolithic enclosure on White Sheet Hill.

White Sheet Hill is rich in prehistoric monuments, including a rare causewayed enclosure, one of the earliest types of British earthworks. This neolithic camp consists of a ring of short banks and ditches built about 5,500 years ago. Evidence suggests prehistoric local farmers met here for markets, fairs or religious ceremonies, and it was probably not built for defence purposes or to enclose village sites, unlike the high ramparts and deep ditches of the adjacent Iron Age hill-fort which dates from 500 BC.

Continue along the track and cross the stile on your right by the information board, Point **B**. Turn left alongside the fence to reach the Iron Age fort. At the trig point, cut across the centre of the fort and bear right along the path on top of the rampart and continue along the scarp edge. Admire the views west across Stourhead Estate to King Alfred's Tower on the skyline and south east across the Blackmore Vale to the Dorset Downs beyond.

Cross a stile at the top of the old quarry and follow the stepped path down through the quarry, bearing left to a stile. Keep left through the car park and follow the track to a gate. Proceed ahead, pass through Beech Clump, Point **C**, and continue on the wide track, crossing two stiles, to reach a gate and the B3092 opposite Drove Lodge. Turn left for 50yds (46m), then take the footpath right through trees to a stile. Walk straight across parkland towards Stourhead House and join your outward route back to the main drive and Walk 43 at Point **7**.

# Westbury White Horse

*An exhilarating downland walk
to a famous white horse.*

DISTANCE *4.25 miles (6.8km)*   MINIMUM TIME *2hrs 30min*

ASCENT/GRADIENT *557ft (170m)* ▲▲▲   LEVEL OF DIFFICULTY +++

PATHS *Field paths and downland tracks, 1 stile*

LANDSCAPE *Downland*

SUGGESTED MAP *OS Explorer 143 Warminster & Trowbridge*

START/FINISH *Grid reference: ST 914523*

DOG FRIENDLINESS *On leads near grazing animals on Combe Bottom,
Bratton Camp and Westbury Hill*

PARKING *Jubilee Hall in Tynings Lane, Bratton, just off B3098*

PUBLIC TOILETS *None on route*

## WALK 45 DIRECTIONS

The most notable feature of
Bratton, a large village in the
shadow of a huge downland
escarpment, is the Church of
St James, arguably one of the most
charming churches in the county.
Reached by a series of steep steps,
and nestling at the base of the
chalk downland, it dates from
about 1400 and is worth the climb
to view the traces of Norman
architecture and the wildly
grinning gargoyles.

Turn right out of the car park
to the B3098. Turn left, then
almost immediately left again up
The Butts. Fork right into Upper
Garston Lane by the Oratory of
St Giles then, just before the lane
dips, take the path left, waymarked

to the church. Descend steps, cross
a brook, then climb steps to the
church gates. Take the narrow path
right and ascend through trees.

When you reach a kissing gate
on your left, turn right along a
waymarked path; go through a
kissing gate and bear left, climbing
steeply up the scarp slope to
the fence at the top. Keep right
alongside the fence, continue
through a gate, then turn right
through a metal gate to follow a
sunken track around the top of
Combe Bottom. At the lane, turn
left uphill and, as the lane bears
left, fork right over a stile on
to the outer rampart of Bratton
Camp. Bear right to follow the
outer rampart path to reach the
Westbury White Horse hill figure.

Westbury Hill rises to the
commanding height of 750ft
(229m) above sea level and forms
the dramatic western edge of
Salisbury Plain. The views are
tremendous, with the scarp slope
dropping into the Vale of Pewsey,
and on the horizon, on a clear day,

### WHERE TO EAT AND DRINK

Refresh yourselves after this
taxing downland walk at the
Duke in Bratton, noted for its
generous home-cooked food,
including excellent Sunday
roasts, and for Moles ales.

## WHAT TO LOOK FOR

Make sure you pause at the viewpoint pillar on Westbury Hill, especially on a clear day, as you will be surprised just how far-reaching the view is. Walk this way in spring and early summer to see the grassy downland summit and slopes alive with chalk loving plants, such as bird's foot trefoil, and butterflies like the chalkhill blue.

of whisky of the same name, was cut by a Mr Gee, steward to Lord Abingdon, in 1778, apparently because he objected to the primitive dog-like creature which had previously existed on Westbury Hill. The White Horse was remodelled in 1853 and restored 20 years later, with its most recent makeover in concrete, courtesy of Westbury Cement Works (the unmistakable industrial complex you can see in the valley below).

you can see across Somerset to the Mendips and the Cotswolds. Dominating the hilltop is Bratton Castle, an Iron Age hill-fort covering 25 acres (10ha) of the plateau and defended by double banks and ditches rising to 35ft (11m). The long barrow inside the fort is a burial mound probably built before 3000 BC.

Cut into the side of the hill, just below the castle ramparts, is Wiltshire's oldest and best known white horse measuring 180ft (55m) long and 108ft (33m) high. This graceful hill figure is believed to have replaced a much earlier and cruder creature which local tradition states was cut in celebration of King Alfred's victory over the Danes at the Battle of Ethundun in AD 878. The present, well-proportioned animal, which is featured on the bottles of a brand

Shortly, leave the rampart and pass through a gate onto Westbury Hill. Keep to the path, passing benches and a viewpoint pillar, and soon reach a track. Turn left, pass the car park entrance and turn right at the T-junction. Pass White Horse Farm and turn left along the track to join the Imber Range Perimeter Path.

This is a 30 mile (48km) trail circumnavigating the Army's largest live firing range in the south of England. For more than 50 years an area of Salisbury Plain 10 miles (16.1km) long and 5 miles (8km) wide has been occupied by the Army and public access has been very limited. Your view south is across the great central plateau, a wild and lonely landscape, full of mystery and a sense of space.

Keep to the track for 0.75 mile (1.2km) to a barn and take the bridle path left through a gate. Follow the track past a copse into a field and keep to the left-hand edge to a gate. Bear right steeply down a sunken track towards Bratton. Go through a gate and descend through trees and keep ahead on reaching a metalled lane. Turn left at the T-junction, then bear left up a cobbled path (The Ball) between cottages. At the road, keep left back to the hall and car park.

## WHILE YOU'RE THERE

Make the short trip east along the B3098 to Edington to see the impressive, cathedral-like Priory Church of St Mary, St Katharine and All Saints. This architectural treasure was completed in 1361 as part of a priory founded by William of Edington, Bishop of Winchester, for Augustinian monks. There is much to marvel at, including a rare wooden screen of 1500 and a fine 17th-century plaster ceiling, so pick up a church guide.

# Corsham – a Wealthy Weaving Town

*Explore this architectural treasure of a town and the adjacent Corsham Park.*

| | |
|---|---|
| DISTANCE 4 miles (6.4km) | MINIMUM TIME 2hrs |
| ASCENT/GRADIENT 114ft (35m) ▲▲▲ | LEVEL OF DIFFICULTY +++ |
| PATHS Field paths and country lanes, 10 stiles | |
| LANDSCAPE Town streets, gently undulating parkland, farmland | |
| SUGGESTED MAP OS Explorer 156 Chippenham & Bradford-on-Avon | |
| START/FINISH Grid reference: ST 871704 | |
| DOG FRIENDLINESS Can be off lead in Corsham Park, except where grazing | |
| PARKING Long-stay car park in Newlands Lane | |
| PUBLIC TOILETS Short-stay car park by shopping precinct | |

Warm, cream-coloured Bath stone characterises this handsome little market town on the southern edge of the Cotswolds. An air of prosperity pervades the streets where the 15th-century Flemish gabled cottages and baroque-pedimented 17th-century Hungerford Almshouses mix with larger Georgian residences. Architectural historian Nikolaus Pevsner wrote: 'Corsham has no match in Wiltshire for the wealth of good houses.' The town owes its inheritance to the once-thriving industries of cloth manufacture and stone quarrying in the 17th and 18th centuries.

## Architectural Delights

Spend some time exploring the heart of the town before setting off across Corsham Park, as many of the fine stone buildings along the High Street, Church Street and Priory Street have been well preserved. Begin your town stroll at the Heritage Centre in the High Street (No 31), where interactive displays and hands-on exhibits present the stories of the weaving industry and quarrying of the golden Bath stone, which was used to create the architectural legacy of the town. In fact, No 31 once belonged to a prosperous 18th-century clothier, and No 70 (now an electrical shop) was the workhouse providing labour for the cloth industry. The Town Hall was formerly the market hall with one storey and open arches before being converted in 1882. North of the post office you will see the unspoilt line of 17th-century weavers' cottages. Known as the Flemish Buildings, this was the centre of the cloth industry where the Flemish weavers settled following religious persecution in their homeland. In Church Street, note the gabled cottages of the 18th-century weavers, with their ornate porches and a door on the first floor for taking in the raw wool.

## Corsham Court – the Methuen Family Home

The finest of the houses is Corsham Court, a splendid Elizabethan mansion built in 1582 on the site of a medieval royal manor. It was bought in 1745 by Paul Methuen, a wealthy clothier and ancestor of the present owner, to house the family's collection of 16th- and 17th-century Italian and Flemish

# CORSHAM

Master paintings and statuary. The house and park you see today are principally the work of 'Capability' Brown, John Nash and Thomas Bellamy. Brown built the gabled wings that house the state rooms and magnificent 72ft (22m) long picture gallery and laid out the park, including the avenues, Gothic bathhouse and the 13-acre (5ha) lake. Round off your walk with a tour of the house. You will see the outstanding collection of more than 140 paintings, including pictures by Rubens, Turner, Reynolds and Van Dyck, fine statuary and bronzes, and the famous collection of English furniture, notably pieces by Robert Adam and Thomas Chippendale. You may recognise the house as the backdrop for the film *The Remains of the Day* (1993) starring Anthony Hopkins.

## WALK 46 DIRECTIONS

❶ Turn left out of the car park, then left again along Post Office Lane to reach the High Street. Turn left, pass the tourist information centre and turn right into Church Street. Pass the impressive entrance to Corsham Court, on your left, and enter St Bartholomew's churchyard.

❷ Follow the path left to a gate and walk ahead to join the main path across Corsham Park. Turn left and walk along the south side

**WHERE TO EAT AND DRINK**

Corsham is well served by pubs, restaurants and cafés, notably The Flemish Weaver pub on the High Street, serving modern food and excellent Bath Ales.

**WHILE YOU'RE THERE**

Visit Sheldon Manor Gardens (3 miles/4.8km north), Wiltshire's oldest inhabited manor house and sole survivor of a deserted medieval village. Dating from 1282, this well-preserved Plantagenet house has been a family home for 700 years and features a 13th-century porch, a 15th-century chapel and beautiful informal terraced gardens.

of the park, passing Corsham Lake, to reach a stile and gate. Keep straight on along a fenced path beside a track to a kissing gate and proceed across a field to a stile and lane.

**3** Turn left, pass Park Farm, a splendid stone farmhouse, on your left and shortly take the waymarked footpath right along a drive to pass Rose and Unicorn House. Cross a stile and follow the right-hand field-edge to a stile, then bear half left to a stone stile in the field corner. Ignore the path arrowed right and head straight across the field to a further stile and lane.

**4** Take the footpath opposite, bearing half left to a stone stile to the left of a cottage. Maintain direction, passing to the right of a spring and go through a field entrance to follow the path along the left-hand side of a field to a stile in the corner. Turn left along the road for 0.5 mile (800m) to reach the A4.

**5** Go through the gate in the wall on your left and follow the worn path right, across the centre of parkland pasture to a metal kissing gate. Proceed ahead to reach a kissing gate on the edge of woodland. Follow the wide path to a further gate and bear half right to a stile.

**6** Keep ahead on a worn path across the parkland and along the field-edge to a gate. Continue to a further gate with fine views right

to Corsham Court. Follow the path right along the field-edge, then where it curves right, bear left to join the path beside the churchyard wall to a stile.

**WHAT TO LOOK OUT FOR**

Note the Folly along Church Street, an artificial ruin, set with church windows, built by Nash in 1800 to hide Ethelred House from Corsham Court. Seek out the grave of Sarah Jarvis behind St Bartholomew's Church; she died in 1703 aged 107 having grown a new set of teeth! A plaque at 38 High Street informs that Sir Michael Tippett, one of Britain's greatest composers, lived there in the 1960s.

**7** Turn left down the avenue of trees to a gate and the town centre, noting the stone almshouses on your left. Turn right along Lacock Road and then right again along the pedestrianised High Street. Turn left back along Post Office Lane to the car park.

# The Longleat Estate

*Combine glorious woodland and parkland walking through the Longleat Estate, and a visit to an opulent Elizabethan mansion.*

---

**DISTANCE** 5.25 miles (8.4km)

**MINIMUM TIME** 2hrs 30min (longer if visiting Longleat attractions)

**ASCENT/GRADIENT** 508ft (155m) ▲▲▲　**LEVEL OF DIFFICULTY** +++

**PATHS** Field, woodland and parkland paths, roads, 4 stiles

**LANDSCAPE** Wooded hillside, village streets, parkland

**SUGGESTED MAP** OS Explorer 143 Warminster & Trowbridge

**START/FINISH** Grid reference: ST 827422

**DOG FRIENDLINESS** On lead through grounds

**PARKING** Heaven's Gate car park, Longleat Estate

**PUBLIC TOILETS** Longleat attractions complex

---

Your first view of Longleat is an unforgettable one. As you stroll down the azalea- and rhododendron-lined path to Heaven's Gate, nothing prepares you for the superb panorama that stretches to the distant Mendip Hills. Central to this composition is Longleat House, an exquisite Elizabethan stone manor in a glorious, wooded, lakeside setting that looks more like a fairy-tale palace from a distance.

Longleat was the first stately home in Britain to open its doors to the public as a commercial proposition, first doing so in 1949, a trend which many would follow. Lions made Longleat famous in 1966 and since then the Marquess of Bath's home has amassed an ever-expanding roll-call of family attractions to keep it viable, including a safari park, hedged mazes, safari boats and a narrow gauge railway. Thankfully, there are also thousands of acres of landscaped parkland and estate woodland to explore, so you can escape the summer crowds and enjoy the wonderful setting.

### Majestic Mansion

Architect and builder Sir John Thynne, an ancestor of the Marquess of Bath, completed the Elizabethan mansion in 1580 on a site chosen for its beauty. The house was revolutionary in its design as it showed no thought for defence, its great bayed walls of stone and mullioned glass windows setting a new trend for Elizabethan architecture.

The splendid exterior is more than matched by the inside. Longleat contains a mixture of furnishings and artefacts reflecting the tastes and interests of the Thynne family throughout the centuries to the flamboyant 7th Marquess of Bath who owns Longleat today. Notable artefacts include a 33ft-long (10m) 16th-century oak shuffle-board, a 17th-century gilt steeplechase cup and a library table commissioned from John Makepeace. Rich 17th-century Flemish tapestries, Genoese velvet and ancient Spanish leather clothe the walls, while painted ceilings, inspired by Italian palace interiors, including the Ducal Palace in Venice, and marble fireplaces ornament the state rooms. A tour will also reveal a fine collection of paintings, from 16th-century portraits and 18th-century Dutch paintings to early Italian pictures and notable hunting scenes. The fully restored Victorian kitchens give an interesting picture of life below stairs.

## 'Artist' Lord Bath

The colourful current Lord Bath began painting in the early 1960s and covered his private rooms in the West Wing with an amazing cycle of paintings. Expressing 'keyhole glimpses of his pysche' are vast murals with satirical and erotic love scenes, while on the staircase hang the portraits of his numerous 'wifelets', or mistresses, in chronological order. Born in 1932, this bearded Bohemian is also a sound businessman who has turned Longleat into a thriving, multi-million pound tourist attraction.

## WALK 47 DIRECTIONS

**1** Cross the road and follow the path into the trees. Disregard the straight track left, bear right and then left along a gravelled path through mixed woodland to double gates and reach the viewpoint at Heaven's Gate.

**2** Facing Longleat, go through the gate in the left-hand corner. In 180yds (165m) at a crossing of paths, turn right, then keep right at a fork and head downhill through woodland to a metalled drive by a thatched cottage. Turn right on to the waymarked bridleway and pass the cottage

# LONGLEAT

WHERE TO EAT AND DRINK

You will find refreshment kiosks and two cafés (Cellar Café is best) within the Longleat complex. For interesting pub food, good ale and wine, stop off at the Bath Arms in Horningsham. Picnic on a bench at Heaven's Gate and enjoy the best view across Longleat.

gate. Now follow the path left, heading downhill close to the woodland edge to reach a lane by The Garden Cottage.

**3** Turn left along White Street to a crossroads and turn right downhill. Ascend past the church to a T-junction and turn right. Turn left opposite the school, following the bridle path up a track and between sheds to a gate. Bear left with the grassy track, pass through two gates and bear slightly right to a gate and stile on the edge of woodland.

**4** Follow the path through the copse and soon bear off right diagonally downhill to a gate. Turn left along the field edge to reach a track. Turn right, go through a gate beside a thatched cottage and follow the metalled lane (Pottle Street). In 200yds (183m), cross the stile on your right and cross the field to a stile and rejoin the lane.

**5** Turn right and follow this quiet lane to a crossroads. Proceed straight across and follow the road through Horningsham village, passing the thatched chapel, to the crossroads opposite the Bath Arms.

**6** Go straight across the crossroads, walk down the estate drive and through the gatehouse arch into Longleat Park. With the magnificent house ahead of you, walk beside the metalled drive with the lakes and weirs to your right. At a T-junction in front of the house, keep ahead to visit the house and follow the path left to reach the other tourist attractions.

**7** For the main route, turn right and walk beside the drive, heading uphill through the Deer Park. Bear left with the drive and climb steeply, then turn sharp right through a wooden gate onto a metalled drive. With beautiful views across the parkland, gently ascend Prospect Hill and reach Heaven's Gate viewpoint. Retrace your steps to the car park.

WHAT TO LOOK FOR

Note the group of pollarded lime trees outside the Bath Arms in Horningsham. Planted in 1793, they are known as the Twelve Apostles. The tomb of Thomas Thynne, 2nd Viscount Weymouth, can be seen in Horningsham churchyard. Figure out the fascinating Sun Maze or the Lunar and Love Labyrinths around the grounds at Longleat.

Visit the oldest free church in England as you stroll through Horningsham. Accessed via a cobbled path, this thatched meeting house was provided by Sir John Thynne in 1566, for the Scottish workmen who built Longleat. Climb Cley Hill (800ft/244m), north of the estate, to see a hill-fort, superb surrounding views and perhaps a UFO, as spotters have regularly met here since the first claimed sighting in 1965. To see the Thynne family tomb, visit the Church of St Peter and St Paul in nearby Longbridge Deverill. Here lies the 1st Viscount Weymouth, shot in Pall Mall in 1714, and the 3rd Viscount, criticised by George II for loving 'nothing but women, cards and strong beer'.

*Overleaf: Longleat House in Wiltshire (Walk 47)*

# A Canal and a Church at Bradford-on-Avon

*Combine a visit to this enchanting riverside town and its surprising Saxon church, with a canalside stroll.*

WALK 48

---

DISTANCE *3.25 miles (5.3km)*   MINIMUM TIME *1hr 45min*

ASCENT/GRADIENT *164ft (50m)* ▲▲   LEVEL OF DIFFICULTY ✦✦✦

PATHS *Tow path, field and woodland paths, metalled lanes*

LANDSCAPE *Canal, river valley, wooded hillsides, town streets*

SUGGESTED MAP *OS Explorer156 Chippenham & Bradford-on-Avon*

START/FINISH *Grid reference: ST 824606*

DOG FRIENDLINESS *On lead through town*

PARKING *Bradford-on-Avon Station car park (charge)*

PUBLIC TOILETS *Station car park*

---

Set in the wooded Avon Valley, Bradford is one of Wiltshire's loveliest towns, combining historical charm, appealing architecture and dramatic topography. It is often likened to a miniature Bath, the town sharing the same honey-coloured limestone, elegant terraces and steep winding streets that rise sharply away from the river. Historically a 'broad ford' across the Avon, the original Iron Age settlement was expanded in turn by the Romans and Saxons, the latter giving Bradford its greatest treasure, St Laurence's Church. The Avon was spanned by a fine stone bridge in the 13th century – two of its arches survive in the present 17th-century structure – and by the 1630s Bradford had grown into a powerful centre for the cloth and woollen industries.

## Wealthy Wool Town

Explore the riverside and the lanes, alleys and flights of steps up the north slope of the town to see beautiful terraces lined with elegant 18th-century merchants' houses with walled gardens, and charming 17th- and 18th-century weavers' cottages, the best examples being located along Newtown, Middle Rank and Tory terraces. The latter is the highest and affords superb views of the town. The wealth needed for all this building came from the manufacture of woollen cloth. In the early 1700s Daniel Defoe, author of *Robinson Crusoe*, commented 'They told me at Bradford that it was no extra-ordinary thing to have clothiers in that county worth from £10,000 to £40,000 per man.' Bradford's medieval prosperity is reflected in the size of the magnificent 14th-century tithe barn at Barton Farm.

With mechanisation, the wool trade moved from individual houses to large water- and steam-driven mills on the banks of the Avon. At the time that the Kennet and Avon Canal was built, in 1810, the town supported around 30 mills, some of which survive today, in various degrees of restoration or disrepair. With the centre of the wool trade shifting north to Yorkshire, the industry declined during the 19th century and the last of the mills closed in 1905. The town is now prosperous once again with tourists and new residents, many commuting to Bath, Bristol and even London.

## Jewel in the Crown

Down by the river, the tiny, bare Saxon Church of St Laurence is the jewel in Bradford's crown. Founded by St Aldhelm, the Abbot of Malmesbury, in AD 700, this present structure dates from the 10th century. For centuries its presence was forgotten. The chancel became a house, the nave a school, and the west wall formed part of a factory building. The true origins and purpose of the site were rediscovered in 1858 and, after careful restoration, it remains one of the best-preserved Saxon churches in England.

## WALK 48 DIRECTIONS

**❶** Walk to the end of the car park, away from the station, and follow the path left beneath the railway and beside the River Avon. Enter Barton Farm Country Park and keep to the path across a grassy area to a junction of paths. With the packhorse bridge right, bear right, then left to pass to the right of the tithe barn to reach the Kennet and Avon Canal.

**❷** Turn right along the tow path, signed to Avoncliff. Cross the bridge over the canal in 0.5 mile (800m) and follow the path right to a footbridge and gate. Proceed along the right-hand field-edge to a further gate, then bear diagonally left uphill away from the canal to a kissing gate.

**❸** Follow the path along the edge of woodland. Keep to this path as it bears left uphill through the trees to reach a metalled lane. Turn right and walk steeply downhill to the canal at Avoncliff.

**❹** Don't cross the aqueduct, instead pass the Mad Hatter Tea Rooms, descend the steps on your right and pass beneath the canal. Keep right by The Cross Guns

and join the tow path towards Bradford-on-Avon. Continue for 0.75 mile (1.2km) to the bridge passed on your outward route.

### WHERE TO EAT AND DRINK

In Bradford, try the Cottage Co-operative Café in Weaver's Walk, the Swan in Church Street and the Canal Tavern or the Lock Inn Canalside Café on Frome Road. The Cross Guns at Avoncliff offers pub food and a riverside garden. The Mad Hatter Tea Rooms serve lunches and teas.

**❺** Bear off left downhill along a metalled track and follow it beside the River Avon back into Barton Farm Country Park. Cross the packhorse bridge and the railway and follow the walled path uphill and right into Barton Orchard. Bear right at the end down the alleyway to Church Street.

**❻** Continue ahead past the Holy Trinity Church and the Church of St Laurence. Cross the footbridge and go through St Margaret's car park to the road. Turn right, then right again to the station car park.

### WHILE YOU'RE THERE

Discover the Bradford's heritage with a visit to the town's fascinating museum. Barton Farm Country Park has craft shops in medieval farm buildings and Bradford's magnificent, tithe barn with its great beams and rafters.

### WHAT TO LOOK OUT FOR

The small, dome-shaped building at the south end of Town Bridge was a lock-up or 'blind house' containing two cells with iron bedsteads for prisoners.

# Through the Frome Valley

*Extend your walk through the beautiful Frome Valley.*
**See map and information panel for Walk 48**

---

**DISTANCE** *3.5 miles (5.7km)*  **MINIMUM TIME** *2hrs*

**ASCENT/GRADIENT** *170ft (52m)* ▲▲▲  **LEVEL OF DIFFICULTY** ✦✦✦

---

## WALK 49 DIRECTIONS
### (Walk 48 Option)

At Avoncliff (point **4** on Walk 48), drop down with the Mad Hatter Tea Rooms on your left, disregard the tow path signs and keep ahead along the track to pass Ancliffe Square. As it veers left, maintain your direction through the gate and trees. Go through a gate and soon walk beside the River Avon to reach another gate. Pass through woodland to a gate, then head across water-meadows to a gate and lane and the River Frome at Freshford, Point **A**.

Turn left, climb a stile on your right and bear half left across the field towards a derelict factory, to a stile and lane. Turn right, walk beside the river and cross the bridge. Continue uphill and take the bridle path left in front of Dunkirk Mill Cottage, Point **B**. Bear right, then take the bridle path left opposite Middle House.

Continue to a gate, keep left down to a track and then turn left. Turn right opposite a house called Whistlers Hollow, to a stile and gate. Keep left through a field to another stile and walk through Friary Wood to a stile. Turn right along the field edge for 0.5 mile (800m) to a stile and lane. Turn left, pass Iford Mill and cross the river bridge to Iford Manor Gardens.

Bear right and walk steeply uphill to a junction, Point **C**.

Turn left along the verge for 0.25 mile (400m) and take the bridle path right, signed 'Upper Westwood'. At a lane, turn right through Upper Westwood. Turn left opposite the telephone box, Point **D** then, where the lane curves left, take the left of two footpaths ahead. Walk downhill through the edge of woodland. Go through a gate, cross a drive and follow the lane left, downhill back to Avoncliff to rejoin Walk 48.

# Tow Path Trail to Bath

*Discover canal architecture
on this tow path walk into Somerset.*

DISTANCE *9.25 miles (14.9km)*  MINIMUM TIME *3hrs 45min*

ASCENT/GRADIENT *Negligible* ▲▲▲  LEVEL OF DIFFICULTY +++

PATHS *Canal tow path*

LANDSCAPE *River valley and urban area*

SUGGESTED MAP *OS Explorers 155 Bristol and Bath;
156 Chippenham & Bradford-on-Avon*

START/FINISH *Grid reference: ST 824606 (on Explorer 156)*

DOG FRIENDLINESS *No real problems; many other dogs on houseboats;
keep under control through Bath*

PARKING *Bradford-on-Avon Station pay-and-display car park*

PUBLIC TOILETS *Bradford-on-Avon Station car park and Bath Spa Station*

## WALK 50 DIRECTIONS

Bradford-on-Avon lies on the Kennet and Avon Canal, which stretches 87 miles (140km) from the River Avon at Bristol to the River Thames at Reading. Now fully restored, the canal offers some of the best-loved walking in Wiltshire. Between Bradford and Bath it passes through steep, wooded hillsides that rise 400ft (122m) above the Avon Valley, arguably the finest natural landscape along the length of the canal. But there is far more than just great scenery for you to savour on this memorable 9.25-mile (14.9km) ramble to

### WHAT TO LOOK OUT FOR
Note the tow rope marks etched into the tight corner of Avoncliff Aqueduct and the two mills below beside the River Avon. Look for the 0.25 mile (400m) posts showing the distance from the River Thames at Reading, and the cast-iron crane at Dundas Wharf.

Bath. You will discover some exceptional canal architecture, notably restored wharves, magnificent aqueducts, a 19th-century pumping station and ornately decorated tunnels.

At Bradford-on-Avon the canal company built two wharves, one below and one above the lock. A lock was required to raise the level of the canal to that of the Wilts and Berks Canal at Semington. On the upper wharf, a stone and timber structure was built and alongside it remains the original dry dock, now in use again.

Walk to the end of the car park away from the station and follow the path left beneath the railway and beside the river. Enter Barton Farm Country Park and keep to the path across a grassy area to an information board. Veer left, ascending, and pass to the right of the tithe barn, using steps to reach the Kennet and Avon Canal. Turn right along the tow path for 1.75 miles (2.8km) to Avoncliff.

# BATH

With great skill, the engineer John Rennie took the canal along the winding Avon Valley crossing the river twice via substantial aqueducts. Avoncliff Aqueduct was built in 1804 to take the canal across the valley to the north side. It is 110yds (100m) long and features three arches, a solid parapet and balustraded ends. The Bath stone has not weathered well and has suffered from casual repair work and patching in brick.

Zig-zag at the Cross Guns to pass beneath the canal. Ascend steps and join the tow path on the opposite side. Proceed for 3 miles (4.8km) to the Dundas Aqueduct.

Perhaps the most impressive of the masonry structures on the canal, Dundas Aqueduct stands as a fitting memorial to the architectural and engineering skill of John Rennie. Built in 1804, this fine classical stone aqueduct carries the canal 64ft (19.5m) above the River Avon on a graceful wide arch spanning 65ft (19.8m) and framed by paired giant pilasters. Brassknocker Basin marks the junction of the Kennet and Avon Canal with the Somerset Coal Canal, opened in 1801 to run 10 miles (16.1km) to the mines at Paulton and Radstock. It was taken over by a railway company and closed in 1898. The first 0.25 mile (400m) was restored between 1986–88 for moorings.

Cross the bridge over the canal and continue for 1.25 miles (2km) to Claverton Pumping Station.

The waterwheel powered pumping station was built at Claverton in 1810 to raise the water from the Avon to the canal and is the only one of its kind on British canals. Now fully restored it is open to the public from April to October at weekends and on Wednesdays (pumping roughly two Sundays each month).

Keep to the tow path through the now very rural Avon Valley, with all eras of transport modes in sight – river, canal, railway and road. Beyond Bathampton, the tow path leads you through the attractive suburbs of Bath, probably the least stressful and least busy route into the heart of the city. Pass through Sydney Gardens, cross the canal in front of Sydney House and continue on the opposite side of the canal. At the bottom of Bathwick Hill, cross the road and canal and continue along the tow path, passing locks to reach the A36.

**WHERE TO EAT AND DRINK**

For Bradford and Avoncliff see Walk 48. Try the excellent Fordside Tea Rooms in a garden beside the canal at Limpley Stoke or the Hop Pole Inn. At Brassknocker Basin there is a café and canal museum. The George at Bathampton offers good food and ale.

Cross the lock gates on your left, drop down steps and pass beneath the road. At lock number seven you'll reach the junction where the canal meets the River Avon. Do not follow the riverside path ahead, instead move left to walk along the pavement and turn right across the footbridge over the Avon to reach Bath Spa Station. Return to Bradford-on-Avon via the half-hourly train service (hourly on Sundays).

# Walking in Safety

All these walks are suitable for any reasonably fit person, but less experienced walkers should try the easier walks first. Route finding is usually straightforward, but you will find that an Ordnance Survey map is a useful addition to the route maps and descriptions.

## RISKS

Although each walk here has been researched with a view to minimising the risks to the walkers who follow its route, no walk in the countryside can be considered to be completely free from risk. Walking in the outdoors will always require a degree of common sense and judgement to ensure that it is as safe as possible.

- Be particularly careful on cliff paths and in upland terrain, where the consequences of a slip can be very serious.

- Remember to check tidal conditions before walking on the seashore.

- Some sections of route are by, or cross, busy roads. Take care and remember traffic is a danger even on minor country lanes.

- Be careful around farmyard machinery and livestock, especially if you have children with you.

- Be aware of the consequences of changes in the weather and check the forecast before you set out. Carry spare clothing and a torch if you are walking in the winter months. Remember the weather can change very quickly at any time of the year, and in moorland and heathland areas, mist and fog can make route finding much harder. Don't set out in these conditions unless you are confident of your navigation skills in poor visibility. In summer remember to take account of the heat and sun; wear a hat and carry spare water.

- On walks away from centres of population you should carry a whistle and survival bag. If you do have an accident requiring the emergency services, make a note of your position as accurately as possible and dial 999.

## COUNTRYSIDE CODE

- Be safe, plan ahead and follow any signs.

- Leave gates and property as you find them.

- Protect plants and animals and take your litter home.

- Keep dogs under close control.

- Consider other people.

For more information visit www.countrysideaccess.gov.uk/things_to_know/countryside_code